£35

CW00392660

LUXURY HOTELS

AFRICA/MIDDLE EAST

edited by Martin Nicholas Kunz

teNeues

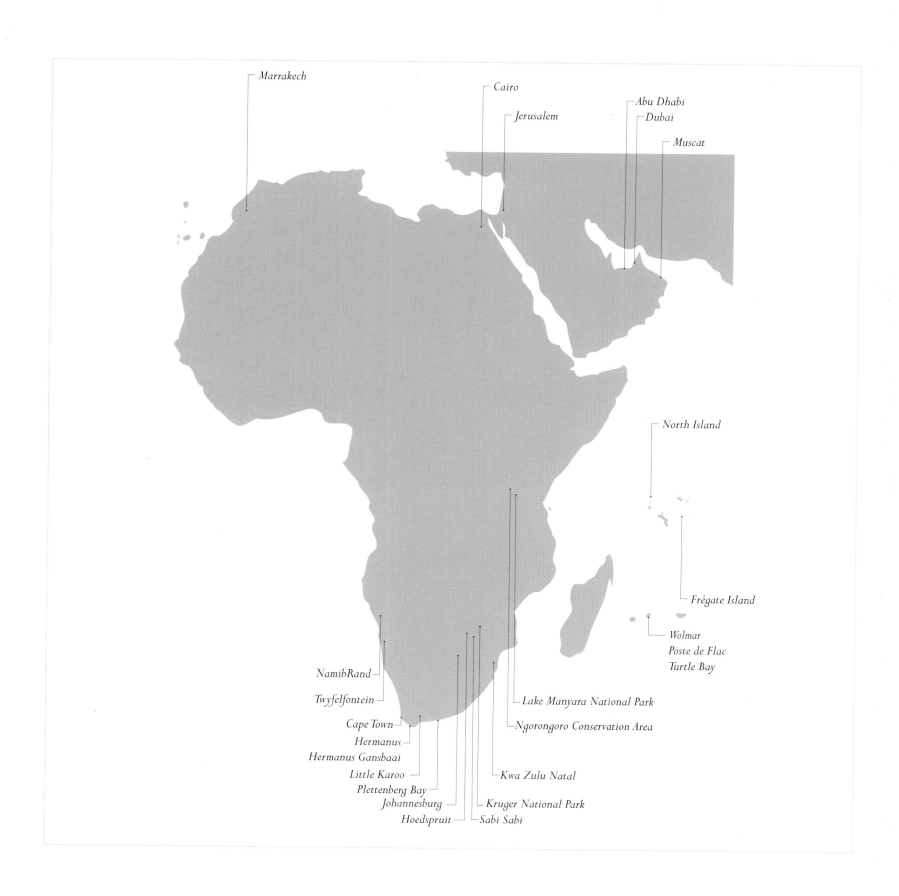

Marrakech

Cairo

Jerusalem

Abu Dhabi

Dubai

Muscat

North Island

Frégate Island

Wolmar
Poste de Flac
Turtle Bay

NamibRand

Twyfelfontein

Cape Town

Hermanus

Hermanus Gansbaai

Little Karoo

Plettenberg Bay

Johannesburg

Hoedspruit

Lake Manyara National Park

Ngorongoro Conservation Area

Kwa Zulu Natal

Kruger National Park

Sabi Sabi

Luxury Hotels
AFRICA / MIDDLE EAST

Introduction 4

Morocco

Marrakech	La Sultana	14
Marrakech	Ksar Char-Bagh	20
Marrakech	Riad Enija	26

Egypt

Cairo	Four Seasons Cairo at The First Residence	32
Cairo	Conrad Cairo	38

Israel

Jerusalem	King David Hotel	42

Oman

Muscat	The Chedi Muscat	48

United Arab Emirates

Abu Dhabi	Emirates Palace Abu Dhabi	54
Dubai	Beit al Bahar Villas	60
Dubai	One&Only Royal Mirage	64
Dubai	Madinat Jumeirah	68
Dubai	Jumeirah Bab Al Shams	74
Dubai	Al Maha Desert Resort & Spa	80

Seychelles

Frégate Island	Frégate Island Private	86
North Island	North Island Lodge	92

Mauritius

Wolmar, Flic en Flac	Taj Exotica Resort & Spa, Mauritius	98
Poste de Flacq	Le Prince Maurice	104
Turtle Bay	The Oberoi Mauritius	110

Tanzania

Ngorongoro Conservation Area	Ngorongoro Crater Lodge	116
Lake Manyara National Park	Lake Manyara Tree Lodge	120

Namibia

NamibRand	Wolwedans	126
NamibRand	Sossuvlei Mountain Lodge	130
Twyfelfontein	Mowani Mountain Camp	134

South Africa

Cape Town	Cape Grace	138
Cape Town	Mount Nelson Hotel	142
Cape Town	The Twelve Apostles Hotel & Spa	146
Hermanus	Birkenhead House	150
Hermanus Gansbaai	Grootbos Nature Reserve	156
Little Karoo	Sanbona Wildlife Reserve	162
Plettenberg Bay	The Plettenberg	166
Plettenberg Bay	Tsala Treetop Lodge	172
Johannesburg	The Grace	178
Johannesburg	Saxon	182
Johannesburg	The Westcliff	188
Kwa Zulu Natal	Phinda Private Game Reserve	192
Kruger National Park	Singita Lebombo Lodge	196
Kruger National Park	Singita Sweni Lodge	202
Hoedspruit	Royal Malewane	206
Sabi Sabi Private Game Reserve	Earth Lodge	212
	Index	218
	Photo Credits	220

About Tents and Palaces

In Africa and the Middle East a new generation of hotels is emerging. Exclusive accommodation in countries like South Africa, Botswana, Tanzania and Kenya is waiting for guests with a personal service, which is not even offered by some five-star hotels in Paris, London and New York. In the United Arab Emirates, hotels are the size of small cities. More than ever before, the Gulf States are breaking away and turning themselves into first-class holiday regions for a sophisticated clientele.

In Africa, luxury has a tradition: it was the adventure-loving, British settlers in the 1920s and 1930s who traveled the continent and set the elegant safari trend by wearing tailor-made hunting outfits, long lace dresses and by carrying a silver tea service in their luggage. Ever since, the "safari" (Kiswahili for "journey") has turned into a lifestyle. Today, lodges, beach hotels and luxury camps are springing up from the dusty earth on the world's poorest continent like desert flowers after the rains. Light aircraft transport travelers to the farthest corners of the massive national park: in exclusive tent camps, guests watch elephants from the bar and the management performs miraculous achievements when freshly caught fish is served deep in the bush. In the South African Phinda Private Game Reserve guests experience African avant-garde. In the glass-enclosed bungalows, modern design and traditional art craftsmanship merges to a daring blend of styles. Along the picturesque "Garden Route" and in Cape Town, guests live in snow-white villas and are looked after as though they are staying with good friends—a personal butler is included. And in the most beautiful Moroccan Riads, they take a rose-petal bath and feel like they are in a fairytale from Thousand and One Nights.

Whilst in Africa, luxury and originality are inextricably linked; it is considered a non-plus-ultra to be so remote from reality in the United Arab Emirates and in the Sultanate of Oman. In the glittering oriental cities, luxury hotels are already worth a journey in themselves. They are magical places that can only be described in superlatives: in the Kempinski Hotel Emirates Palace in Abu Dhabi, the largest of the seven Sheikdoms, the royal suites measure 1,200 square meters. 12,000 craftsmen worked around the clock for two and a half years for this gigantic project. The Al Maha Desert Resort in Dubai is the first Arabian Eco-Resort, a blossoming oasis in traditional Bedouin style. And for the new Madinat Jumeirah, the owners built what is virtually a small lagoon city, right on the fine sandy beach. Some might think that's over the top. But the glamorous style is a success: the Gulf States have travel destinations that represent one of the most dynamic tourist markets in the world. The majestic Sheikdoms breaking away from oil wealth and tradition offer a refined mix of Arabian ambiance, spectacular architecture and perfect luxury.

The book invites you to take a look behind the tent layouts, mahogany doors and the mosaic decorations of gateways to discover a new era of luxury holiday destinations in hospitable countries. It guides you, just like an impressive and illustrated journey, to the most exclusive hideaways on the African continent and in the Middle East—far away from mass tourism.

Camilla Péus

Von Zelten und Palästen

In Afrika und im Mittleren Osten wächst eine neue Hotelgeneration heran. Nobelunterkünfte in Ländern wie Südafrika, Botsuana, Tansania und Kenia warten mit einem persönlichen Service auf, den selbst manches Fünf-Sterne-Hotel in Paris, London und New York nicht bietet. In den Vereinigten Arabischen Emiraten haben Hotels Ausmaße von Kleinstädten. Die Golfstaaten befinden sich mehr denn je im Aufbruch und entwickeln sich zu erstklassigen Urlaubsregionen für Anspruchsvolle.

Luxus hat in Afrika Tradition: Es waren die Abenteuer liebenden, britischen Siedler, die in den 20er und 30er Jahren in maßgeschneiderten Jagdanzügen, langen Spitzenkleidern und mit silbernem Teeservice im Gepäck den Kontinent bereisten und den eleganten Safari-Stil prägten. Seitdem hat sich die „Safari" (Kisuaheli für Reise) zu einem Lebensstil entwickelt. Heute schießen auf dem ärmsten Kontinent der Erde Lodges, Beachhotels und Luxuscamps aus dem staubigen Boden wie Wüstenblumen nach der Regenzeit. Kleinflugzeuge transportieren Reisende in die entlegendsten Winkel der riesigen Nationalparks: In noblen Zeltcamps beobachten Gäste Elefanten von der Bar aus und das Management vollbringt Wunderleistungen, wenn tief im Busch fangfrischer Fisch serviert wird. Im südafrikanischen Phinda Private Game Reserve erleben Gäste afrikanische Avantgarde. In den rundum verglasten Bungalows verschmelzen modernes Design und traditionelles Kunsthandwerk zu einem gewagten Stilmix. An der malerischen „Gardenroute" und in Kapstadt wohnen Gäste in blitzend weißen Villen und werden umsorgt wie bei guten Freunden – persönlicher Butler inbegriffen. Und in den schönsten marokkanischen Riads fühlt man sich bei einem Bad in Rosenblättern wie in einem Märchen aus Tausendundeiner Nacht.

Während in Afrika Luxus und Ursprünglichkeit untrennbar miteinander verbunden sind, gilt in den Vereinigten Arabischen Emiraten und im Sultanat Oman das Realitätsferne als Nonplusultra. Die Luxushotels in den Glitzerstädten des Orients sind schon für sich eine Reise wert. Es sind magische Orte, die sich nur in Superlativen beschreiben lassen: Im Kempinski Hotel Emirates Palace in Abu Dhabi, dem größten der sieben Scheichtümer, sind die Royal Suiten 1.200 Quadratmeter groß. Für das gigantische Projekt haben 12.000 Handwerker 24 Stunden am Tag zweieinhalb Jahre lang gearbeitet. Das Al Maha Desert Resort in Dubai ist das erste arabische Eco-Resort, eine blühende Oase im traditionellen Beduinen-Stil. Und für das neue Madinat Jumeirah haben die Betreiber gleich eine kleine Lagunenstadt direkt am feinsandigen Strand errichtet. Übertrieben, mag mancher denken. Doch der glamouröse Stil kommt an: Die Reiseziele in den Golfstaaten gehören zu den dynamischsten Touristenmärkten weltweit. Die majestätischen Scheichtümer im Aufbruch zwischen Öl und Tradition bieten einen raffinierten Mix aus arabischem Ambiente, spektakulärer Architektur und perfektem Luxus.

Das Buch lädt Sie ein, hinter Zeltplanen, Mahagonitüren und mosaikverzierte Portale zu blicken und eine neue Ära luxuriöser Urlaubsziele in gastfreundlichen Ländern zu entdecken. Einer eindrucksvoll bebilderten Reise gleich, führt es Sie zu den exklusivsten Hideaways des afrikanischen Kontinents und des Mittleren Ostens – fernab des Massentourismus.

Camilla Péus

Du Tentes et du Palais

Une nouvelle génération d'hôtels se développe en Afrique et au Moyen Orient. Dans des pays tels que l'Afrique du Sud, le Botswana, la Tanzanie et le Kenya, des héberge-ments raffinés proposent un service personnel que même certains hôtels cinq étoiles à Paris, Londres et New York n'offrent pas. Dans les Emirats Arabes Unis, les hôtels ont les dimensions de petites villes. Les états du Golfe sont plus que jamais en plein essor et en passe de devenir des destinations de vacances de première classe pour une clientèle exigeante.

L'Afrique a une tradition de luxe : ce sont les colons britanniques amoureux d'aventures qui, sillonnant le continent dans les années 20 et 30 en costumes de chasse taillés sur mesure, en longues robes à dentelle, avec le service à thé en argent dans leurs bagages, ont forgé l'élégant style safari. Le « safari » (voyage en swahili) est devenu depuis un mode de vie. Aujourd'hui poussent sur le continent le plus pauvre du monde des lodges, des Beach Hôtels, des camps de luxe comme les fleurs du désert après la pluie. Des avions petits porteurs emportent les voyageurs dans les coins les plus reculés d'immenses parcs nationaux : dans de confortables campements, les hôtes observent les éléphants, accoudés au bar, et les organisateurs réalisent des miracles pour servir, en plein bush, des poissons fraîchement pêchés. En Afrique du Sud, dans la Phinda Private Game Reserve, les hôtes font l'expérience de l'avant-garde africaine. Les bungalows entourés de baies vitrées associent design moderne et artisanat local dans un audacieux mélange de style. Sur la pittoresque « Garden Route » et à Cape Town, les visiteurs sont hébergés dans des villas d'un blanc éclatant et choyés comme de bons amis — avec un majordome à leur service. Dans les plus beaux riads marocains, dans un bain de pétales de rose, l'hôte vit comme dans un conte des Mille et Une Nuits.

Tandis qu'en Afrique, luxe et authenticité sont indissociables, les Emirats Arabes Unis et le Sultanat d'Oman considèrent l'évasion hors de la réalité comme le nec plus ultra. Les hôtels de luxe des scintillantes villes d'Orient valent le déplacement à eux seuls. Ce sont des lieux magiques que seuls des superlatifs peuvent décrire. Au Kem-pinski Hotel Emirates Palace à Abou Dhabi, le plus grand des sept émirats, les suites royales font 1200 mètres carrés. Pour ce gigantesque projet, 12 000 artisans ont travaillé jour et nuit pendant deux ans et demi. Le Al Maha Desert Resort à Dubai est le premier resort écologique arabe, une oasis fleurissante dans le style traditionnel des bédouins. Et pour le nouveau Madinat Jumeirah, les opérateurs ont construit une petite cité lacustre directement au bord de la plage de sable fin. Exagéré, penseront certains. Pourtant ce style glamour a du succès. Les destinations vers les états du Golfe constituent les marchés touristiques les plus dynamiques. Les majestueux émirats prospérant entre pétrole et tradition offrent un mélange raffiné d'ambiance arabe, d'architecture spectaculaire et de luxe parfait.

Ce livre vous invite à regarder derrière les tentures des campements, les portes en acajou et les portails ornés de mosaïques et à découvrir une nouvelle ère de destinations de vacances luxueuses dans des pays hospitaliers. Semblable à un voyage aux illustrations impressionnantes, il vous emmène dans les paradis cachés les plus exclusifs du continent africain et du Moyen Orient — loin du tourisme de masse.

Camilla Péus

Acerca de Carpas y Palacios

En África y en el Oriente Medio está surgiendo una nueva generación de hoteles. Residencias lujosas en países como Sudáfrica, Botswana, Tanzania y Kenia esperan a sus huéspedes con un servicio personal que algunos hoteles de cinco estrellas de París, Londres y Nueva York, no pueden ofrecer. En los Emiratos Árabes Unidos, los hoteles se asemejan a pequeñas ciudades por sus dimensiones. Los estados del Golfo se encuentran en plena expansión y están evolucionando hacia destinos vacacionales de primera categoría para los más exigentes.

El lujo tiene tradición en África: los amantes de las aventuras, los colonos británicos, fueron los que viajaron por el continente durante las décadas de 1920 y 1930 vestidos con trajes de caza a medida, largos vestidos de encajes y servicios de té de plata en las maletas, creando así el estilo elegante de safari. Desde entonces, el safari (viaje en kisuaheli) ha evolucionado hasta convertirse en un estilo de vida. En la actualidad, los lodges, los hoteles de playa y los campamentos de lujo surgen en el polvoriento suelo de los continentes más pobres como flores del desierto después de las lluvias. Pequeños aviones trasladan a los viajeros hasta los rincones más recónditos de los inmensos parques nacionales. En los elegantes campamentos, los huéspedes observan a los elefantes desde el bar, y la dirección del hotel realiza milagros cuando se sirve pescado recién capturado en la profundidad del bosque. En la Phinda Private Game Reserve, los huéspedes experimentan la modernidad africana. En los bungalows completamente acristalados, el diseño tradicional se funde con la artesanía tradicional creando una atrevida mezcla de estilos. En la pintoresca *garden route* y en la Ciudad del Cabo, los huéspedes se alojan en villas de blanco nuclear y son atendidos como si estuvieran en la casa de unos buenos amigos, con mayordomo particular incluido. Y en los riad, el visitante se siente como en un cuento de las Mil y una noches cuando toma un baño con pétalos de rosa.

Mientras que en África el lujo y el carácter primitivo son inseparables, en los Emiratos Árabes Unidos y en la sultanía de Oman, el distanciamiento de la realidad es lo máximo. Sólo los hoteles de lujo en las resplandecientes ciudades del Oriente hacen que el viaje merezca la pena. Son lugares mágicos que sólo pueden describirse en grado superlativo: en el Kempinski Hotel Emirates Palace, en Abu Dhabi, el mayor de los siete palacios del jeque, están alojadas las suites reales, de 1200 metros cuadrados. En la construcción de este gigantesco proyecto participaron 12 000 obreros, que trabajaron en turnos 24 horas al día durante dos años y medio. El Al Maha Desert Resort en Dubai es el primer Eco Resort árabe, un exuberante oasis en el tradicional estilo beduino. Y para el nuevo Madinat Jumeirah, los propietarios construyeron una pequeña ciudad a orillas de una laguna con una playa de fina arena. Algunos pensarán que todo esto es exagerado. Sin embargo, este glamouroso estilo tiene una buena acogida: Los destinos vacacionales en los estados del Golfo representan uno de los mercados turísticos más dinámicos del mundo. Los majestuosos palacios del jeque entre el petróleo y la tradición ofrecen una sofisticada mezcla entre el ambiente árabe, una arquitectura espectacular y el lujo perfecto.

El libro le invita a asomarse detrás de las tiendas, de las puertas de caoba y de los portales decorados con mosaicos, para descubrir la nueva era de los destinos vacacionales del lujo en unos países hospitalarios. Un impresionante viaje ilustrado con fotografías le conducirá a los escondites más exclusivos del continente africano y del Oriente Medio, lejos del turismo de masas.

Camilla Péus

Di Tendi e di Palazzi

In Africa e nel Medio Oriente cresce e si sviluppa una nuova generazione di alberghi: alloggi signorili in paesi come il Sudafrica, il Botswana, la Tanzania, la Repubblica del Kenya offrono un servizio individuale che non propongono neanche certi hotel cinque stelle a Parigi, Londra e New York. Negli Emirati Arabi Uniti gli alberghi hanno dimensioni di cittadine. Gli Stati del Golfo si destano sempre di più e stanno per diventare gli offerenti per eccellenza di vacanze di prima classe per persone esigenti.

In Africa il lusso ha tradizione: furono infatti quei coloni britannici, amanti delle avventure, che negli anni 20 e 30 visitarono il continente in tenuta da caccia confezionata su misura, vestiti di lunghi abiti di pizzo e con i servizi da tè in argento nei bagagli, a dare la loro impronta all'elegante stile safari. Da allora il "safari" (che in suahili significa viaggio), è andato evolvendosi fino a diventare uno stile di vita. Nel continente più povero della terra nascono oggi dal terreno polveroso lodges, beach hotels e camps di lusso come fiori nel deserto dopo la stagione delle piogge. Aerei da turismo trasportano viaggiatori negli angoli più remoti dei giganteschi parchi nazionali: in eleganti campi tendati gli ospiti osservano dal bar gli elefanti e il management compie veri e propri miracoli quando fa servire nel cuore della foresta vergine pesce appena preso. Nel Phinda Private Game Reserve gli ospiti vengono a contatto con l'avanguardia africana. Nei bungalow a vetri il design moderno si fonde con il tradizionale artigianato artistico formando un'azzardata mescolanza di stili. Lungo la pittoresca Garden Route e a Città del Capo gli ospiti abitano in ville bianchissime e vengono accolti come si accolgono i buoni amici – maggiordomo personale compreso. E facendo il bagno in mezzo ai petali di rose nei più bei riads marocchini ci si sente come in una delle fiabe delle Mille e una notte.

Mentre in Africa lusso e genuina naturalezza sono inseparabilmente legati fra di loro, negli Emirati Arabi Uniti e nel Sultanato dell'Oman star fuori dalla realtà è il non plus ultra dei modi di vivere. Gli alberghi di lusso nelle scintillanti città dell'Oriente valgono già di per sé un viaggio. Sono luoghi magici che si lasciano descrivere solo con superlativi: nell'Hotel Kempinski Emirates Palace ad Abu Dhabi, il più grande dei sette sceiccati, gli appartamenti "Royal Suite" sono grandi 1200 metri quadrati. Per il gigantesco progetto hanno lavorato 12 000 artigiani 24 ore al giorno per due anni e mezzo. L'Al Maha Desert Resort a Dubai è il primo resort eco-turistico arabo, un'oasi fiorente nello stile tipicamente beduino. E per il nuovo Madinat Jumeirah i gestori hanno persino eretto una piccola città laguna direttamente lungo la spiaggia dalla sabbia finissima. Forse c'è chi pensa che sia esagerato, però lo stile affascinante coglie nel segno: i viaggi negli Stati del Golfo sono uno dei mercati turistici più dinamici di tutto il mondo. Gli sceiccati maestosi, che si sono messi in cammino tra petrolio e tradizione, offrono una raffinata mescolanza tra ambiente arabo, spettacolare architettura e lusso perfetto.

Il libro vi invita a dare uno sguardo dietro ai tendoni, alle porte in mogano e ai portali decorati con mosaici e a scoprire una nuova era di mete di viaggi per vacanze di lusso in paesi ospitali. Alla pari di un viaggio illustrato di grande effetto, il libro vi trasporta ai più esclusivi hideaways del continente africano e del Medio Oriente – lontano dal turismo di massa.

Camilla Péus

La Sultana

Marrakech, Morocco

La Sultana offers its guests a first-hand experience of Marrakech's magic: the hotel is in a majestic location in the heart of the Medina—right next to the Saadian tombs—and it celebrates luxury. Inside the rooms, you can marvel at the filigree, ornate arches and the sparkle of highly polished marble, hand-woven carpets and airy curtains, valuable art and specially selected accessories. The palace has 21 suites, three restaurants with an oriental as well as Mediterranean menu and a state-of-the-art spa. A fascinating panorama of the city is possible from its roof terrace.

La Sultana lässt seine Gäste die Magie von Marrakesch ganz unmittelbar erleben: Das Hotel thront im Herzen der Medina – direkt neben der Grabanlage der Saadier – und zelebriert den Luxus. In den Räumen kann man filigran verzierte Bögen und auf Hochglanz polierten Marmor, handgewebte Teppiche und luftige Vorhänge, wertvolle Kunst und ausgesuchte Accessoires bewundern. Der Palast besitzt 21 Suiten, drei Restaurants mit orientalischer sowie mediterraner Karte und ein Spa der Superlative. Von seiner Dachterrasse aus bietet sich ein faszinierendes Panorama der Stadt.

La Sultana fait vivre directement à ses hôtes la magie de Marrakech : l'hôtel trônant au cœur de la Médina – à quelques pas des tombeaux Saadiens – est une ode au luxe. Dans ces pièces, l'hôte peut admirer des arcs ornés en filigrane et du marbre poli, des tapis tissés à la main et des rideaux aériens, de précieuses œuvres d'art et des accessoires choisis. Le palais compte 21 suites, trois restaurants avec cuisine orientale et méditerranéenne et un Spa exceptionnel. La terrasse panoramique offre une vue fascinante sur toute la ville.

La Sultana permite a sus huéspedes experimentar en primera persona la magia de Marrakech: El hotel, pura celebración del lujo, reina en el corazón de la Medina y está situado justo al lado de las Tumbas Saadianas. En sus habitaciones la mirada se pierde entre arcos ricamente adornados con filigranas, alfombras tejidas a mano vaporosas cortinas que se deslizan por el pulido màrmol, piezas artísticas de gran valor y los más exquisitos accesorios. El palacio posee 21 suites, tres restaurantes con cartas orientales y mediterráneas, y un exclusivo balneario. Desde la terraza de la azotea se disfruta de una fascinante vista panorámica sobre la ciudad.

La Sultana lascia avvertire sulla pelle ai suoi ospiti in modo diretto ed immediato la magìa di Marrakech. L'albergo troneggia nel cuore della Medina – direttamente accanto al complesso delle Tombe Saadiane – e celebra il lusso. Nelle camere si possono ammirare archi decorati con filigrana e marmo lucidato a specchio, tappeti tessuti a mano e tende ariose, arte preziosa e accessori ricercati. Il palazzo ha 21 suites, 3 ristoranti con carta per la scelta di pietanze orientali e mediterranee e una SPA eccellente. Dalla terrazza sul tetto si presenta un affascinante panorama della città.

The fabulous rooms revive the atmosphere of 1,001 Nights—and the flair of the former Riads. By day and night, an unforgettable view opens up from the roof terrace over the rooftops of Marrakech.

Die prachtvollen Zimmer lassen die Atmosphäre von 1001 Nacht wieder aufleben – und das Flair ehemaliger Riads. Von der Dachterrasse aus eröffnet sich tagsüber und nachts ein unvergesslicher Blick über die Dächer von Marrakesch.

Les merveilleuses chambres font revivre l'atmosphère des Mille et Une Nuits – ainsi que l'ambiance des anciens riads. De la terrasse panoramique s'ouvre de jour comme de nuit une vue inoubliable sur les toits de Marrakech.

Las lujosas habitaciones evocan la atmósfera de las Mil y una noches y el encanto del antiguo riad. Tanto por el día como por la noche, delante de la terraza de la azotea se extiende una inolvidable vista de los tejados de Marrakech.

Le meravigliose camere fanno tornare a vivere l'atmosfera di Mille e una notte – e il fascino dei riad di una volta. Dalla terrazza sul tetto si offre di giorno e di notte una vista indimenticabile sui tetti di Marrakech.

Each suite was individually designed—hand-carved cedar wood decorates the walls of the rooms. The designer furniture on the gallery around the typical inner courtyard brings a touch of Africa to Morocco.

Jede Suite wurde individuell gestaltet – handgeschnitztes Zedernholz ziert die Wände der Räume. Die Designermöbel auf der Empore rund um den typischen Innenhof bringen einen Hauch Afrika nach Marokko.

Chaque suite a été personnalisée par sa décoration – du cèdre sculpté orne les murs des chambres. Les meubles de designers sur la galerie entourant le typique patio apportent le souffle de l'Afrique au Maroc.

Cada suite ha sido decorada de forma individual y las paredes están adornadas con madera de cedro trabajada a mano. Los muebles de diseño dispuestos en la galería y en los laterales del patio interior, traen reminiscencias de África a Marruecos.

Ogni suite è stata personalizzata – legno di cedro intagliato a mano orna le pareti delle camere. I mobili di design sulla galleria attorno al tipico cortile interno portano un alito di Africa in Marocco.

The baths are a dream in marble. Almost five tons of the white and precious stone take care of pure luxury inside the hotel. In true Moroccan style, mosaics made of thousands of brightly colored tiny discs decorate the arches of the patio.

Die Bäder sind ein Traum aus Marmor. Fast fünf Tonnen des weißen und wertvollen Steins sorgen im Haus für Luxus pur. Ganz nach marokkanischer Tradition schmücken Mosaike aus tausenden von bunten Plättchen die Bögen des Patios.

Les salles de bains sont un rêve en marbre. Quelque cinq tonnes de cette précieuse pierre blanche confèrent son luxe à cet établissement. Fidèles à la tradition marocaine, des mosaïques constituées de milliers de petits carreaux multicolores décorent les arcs du patio.

Los baños son un sueño de mármol. Casi cinco toneladas de esta valiosa piedra blanca simbolizan el lujo de la casa. Siguiendo la tradición marroquí, mosaicos de miles de fragmentos coloridos decoran los arcos del patio.

I bagni sono bagni da sogno in marmo. Quasi cinque tonnellate della pietra bianca e pregiata fanno sì che si senta puro lusso in tutti gli ambienti. Mosaici composti di migliaia di tessere variamente colorate ornano gli archi del patio in perfetta sintonia con la tradizione marocchina.

Ksar Char-Bagh

Marrakech, Morocco

The palatial façade of Ksar Char-Bagh already hints at what awaits the guest inside. Behind the gates, an exclusive gem is revealed, influenced by Moorish splendor: pillars, arches and arabesques, whose graceful features are reminiscent of the Alhambra. Additionally, in typical Arabian style, streams and pathways cross extensive gardens. The ambiance is exotic and in stately style. So, there is no shortage of either hammam made out of marble or generously sized suites. As a result, the French chef is also standing by in the Ksar Char-Bagh with Mediterranean-inspired luxury cuisine.

Schon die palastartige Fassade von Ksar Char-Bagh lässt erahnen, was den Gast im Inneren erwartet. Hinter den Toren öffnet sich ein exklusives Kleinod, geprägt von maurischem Prunk: Säulen, Bögen und Arabesken, deren Anmut an die Alhambra erinnern. Dazu weitläufige Gärten, in typisch arabischer Manier durchzogen von Wasserläufen und Pfaden. Ein Ambiente mit exotisch herrschaftlichem Gestus. So mangelt es weder an einem Hammam aus Marmor noch an ausladend großen Suiten. Folglich wartet der französische Chefkoch im Ksar Char-Bagh auch mit einer mediterran angehauchten Luxusküche auf.

La façade de palais du Ksar Char-Bagh permet déjà à l'hôte de deviner ce qui l'attend à l'intérieur. Les portes s'ouvrent sur un bijou exclusif inspiré de l'art mauresque : colonnes, arcs et arabesques dont le charme rappelle l'Alhambra. Auquel s'ajoutent de vastes jardins de pure tradition arabe où se croisent canaux et chemins. Une atmosphère à l'expression seigneuriale exotique. Où ne manquent ni le hammam de marbre ni les grandes et larges suites. Le chef cuisinier français du Ksar Char-Bagh prépare une cuisine raffinée aux saveurs méditerranéennes.

La fachada palaciega de Ksar Char-Bagh deja entrever lo que le espera al huésped en el interior. Detrás de sus puertas se abre una exclusiva joya de marcada suntuosidad moro: columnas, arcos y arabescos cuyas graciosas líneas recuerdan a la Alhambra, además de extensos jardines en el típico estilo árabe recorridos por acequias y caminos. Un ambiente con una exótica actitud señorial donde es posible disfrutar de un hamman de mármol y de unas amplias habitaciones. En el Ksar Char-Bagh, el cocinero jefe francés sirve a los huéspedes una cocina de lujo inspirada en la gastronomía mediterránea.

La sola facciata di Ksar Char-Bagh, simile a quella di un palazzo, lascia già prevedere quello che aspetta l'ospite all'interno. Dietro alle porte si presentano preziosità caratterizzate da sfarzo moresco: colonne, archi, arabeschi, la cui elegante grazia portano il pensiero al palazzo dell'Alhambra. Inoltre giardini ampi e spaziosi alla tipica maniera araba attraversati da corsi d'acqua e sentieri. Un ambiente dal tono altamente esotico-signorile. Non mancano infatti nè l'Hammam in marmo nè grandi e ampie suites. Il capocuoco francese del Ksar Char-Bagh, quindi, offre anche una cucina lusso, cioè pietanze prelibate e squisite con un tocco mediterraneo.

*The **French** owners knew how to combine ancient Arabian architecture with contemporary styling.*

*Die **französischen** Besitzer haben es verstanden, alte arabische Architektur mit heutiger Stilistik zu vereinen.*

*Les **propriétaires** français ont su conjuguer architecture arabe antique et style moderne.*

*Los **dueños** franceses han sabido unir la antigua arquitectura árabe con el estilo actual.*

*I **proprietari** francesi hanno saputo unire l'antica architettura araba con lo stile odierno.*

In the "harems", the palace's twelve suites, space means everything: one way for the exclusive interior to make an even bigger impact.

In den „Harims", den zwölf Suiten des Palastes, bedeutet Raum haben alles: Das exklusive Interieur kommt so noch besser zur Geltung.

Dans les « Harims », les douze suites du palais, avoir de l'espace revêt une grande importance : les somptueux intérieurs n'en sont que davantage mis en valeur.

En las doce suites, "harim", de este palacio, disponer de espacio lo es todo porque en él resalta, aun mejor, el exclusivo interior.

Negli "harim" — le dodici suites del palazzo — lo spazio è tutto: così risalta ancora di più l'interno elegante e raffinato.

Places, *which are worthy of a palace: the in-house pool, a generously sized dining table and an apartment with a private terrace and pool.*

Orte, *die einem Palast würdig sind: der Pool des Hauses, ein großzügiger Esstisch und ein Apartment mit eigener Terrasse und Pool.*

Des endroits *dignes d'un palais: la piscine de l'établissement, une table de salle à manger de grand style et un appartement avec terrasse et bassin privatifs.*

Lugares *dignos de un palacio: la piscina de la casa, la amplia mesa del comedor y un apartamento con terraza y piscina privadas.*

Ampiezza *degna di un palazzo: la piscina della casa, un grande tavolo da pranzo e un appartamento con terrazza e piscina a sé.*

Riad Enija

Marrakech, Morocco

Once, a silk trader lived in this Riad with his 60-strong family—today, the property is one of Marrakech's most beautiful privately owned accommodation. It consists of two century-old buildings, which have been expertly restored with a love of detail—the mosaics, murals and wood carvings gleam in their old glory. The Riad has twelve double rooms with bathrooms; and each room is furnished in a different and opulent style. You also feel like you are in a fairytale in the garden and on the patios, which are illuminated at night by candlelight.

Einst lebte ein Seidenhändler mit seiner 60-köpfigen Familie in diesem Riad – heute ist das Anwesen eine der schönsten Privatunterkünfte von Marrakesch. Es besteht aus zwei jahrhundertealten Gebäuden, die mit viel Sachverstand und Liebe zum Detail renoviert wurden – die Mosaiken, Malereien und Holzarbeiten strahlen in alter Pracht. Zum Riad gehören zwölf Doppelzimmer mit Bad; alle unterschiedlich und opulent eingerichtet. Wie in einem Märchen fühlt man sich auch im Garten und in den Patios, die abends von Kerzen erleuchtet werden.

Jadis vivait dans ce riad un négociant en soie avec les 60 membres de sa famille – aujourd'hui, c'est une des plus belles maisons d'hôtes de Marrakech. Elle est constituée de deux bâtiments vieux de plusieurs siècles ans rénovés avec une grande expertise et l'amour des détails – les mosaïques, les peintures et les boiseries ont retrouvé leur magnificence. La demeure comprend douze chambres doubles avec salle de bains, toutes différemment aménagées avec opulence. Le jardin et les patios éclairés le soir par des bougies sont également une source d'émerveillement.

En este riad vivió un comerciante de seda con su familia, de 60 miembros. Hoy, este lugar es uno de los alojamientos privados más bellos de Marrakech. Está compuesto por dos edificios centenarios reformados con gran pericia y atención por los detalles: los mosaicos, las pinturas y las tallas de madera vuelven a brillar en su antiguo esplendor. El riad alberga doce habitaciones dobles con cuarto de baño, todas ellas decoradas de forma diferente y fastuosa. El jardín y los patios, alumbrados con velas por la tarde, trasladan al visitante a un mundo de fantasía.

Una volta viveva un commerciante in seta con la sua famiglia di 60 persone in questo riad – oggi la casa signorile è uno degli alloggi privati più belli di Marrakech. Consta di due edifici secolari che sono stati restaurati con molta competenza e cura anche nei dettagli – i mosaici, i dipinti ed i lavori in legno emanano l'antico splendore. Il riad ha dodici camere doppie con bagno, tutte arredate in modo fastoso e differenti fra di loro. Anche nel giardino e nei patio, che di sera sono illuminati da candele, ci si sente come in una favola.

Everywhere, oriental and western style is combined. Filigree mosaics and precious textiles still remind you today of the previous owner—a famous silk trader.

Überall verbinden sich orientalischer und westlicher Stil. Filigrane Mosaike und kostbare Stoffe erinnern noch heute an den einstigen Hausherren – einen berühmten Seidenhändler.

Partout se combinent style oriental et occidental. Les mosaïques en filigrane et les précieuses étoffes rappellent aujourd'hui encore le propriétaire d'antan – un célèbre négociant en soie.

En todos los lugares, el estilo oriental se fusiona con el occidental. Mosaicos de filigrana y preciosos paños recuerdan aún hoy al antiguo propietario, un famoso comerciante de sedas.

Dappertutto si fondono lo stile orientale e occidentale. Mosaici di fattura fine e stoffe preziose fanno pensare ancora oggi al padrone di casa di allora – un famoso commerciante in seta.

In the "Lion Suite" flowing fabrics and striking patterns are predominant. The room also has a private veranda. At night, the inner courtyard becomes a symphony of lights—and the Riad Enija temporarily turns into a private palace.

In der „Lion Suite" dominieren fließende Stoffe und auffallende Muster. Zum Zimmer gehört auch eine eigene Veranda. Abends wird der Innenhof zu einer Sinfonie aus Lichtern — und der Riad Enija zum privaten Palast auf Zeit.

Dans la « Suite Lion » ce sont les étoffes fluides et les motifs originaux qui dominent. La chambre dispose également d'une terrasse privée. Le soir s'élève du patio une symphonie de couleurs — et le Riad Enija se transforme pour un instant en palais privé.

En la "Suite Lion" dominan los tejidos ligeros y los llamativos dibujos. La habitación dispone de una terraza privado. Al atardecer, el patio interior se convierte en una sinfonía de luces y el Riad Enija se transforma, por un tiempo, en un palacio privado.

Nella "Lion Suite" predominano stoffe fluenti e motivi vistosi. La camera ha anche una veranda a sé. La sera il cortile interno si trasforma in una sinfonia di luci — e il Riad Enijasi diventa per un determinato tempo un palazzo privato.

Blue Hour: *In the "Anemone Room" the bath is the absolute highlight. Here, you can relax in a bathtub with golden feet. The "Pan Room" on the first floor lives from golden-colored accents and spots of color in various blue tones.*

Blaue Stunde: *Im „Anemone Room" ist das Bad das absolute Highlight. Hier entspannt man in einer Wanne mit Goldfüßen. Der „Pan Room" im ersten Stock lebt von goldfarbenen Akzenten und Farbtupfern in verschiedenen Blautönen.*

L'heure bleue: *dans la « Chambre Anémone » la salle de bains constitue l'attraction absolue. On s'y relaxe dans une baignoire aux pieds en or. La chambre « Pan » au premier étage est ponctuée de couleurs dorées et de touches de différents tons de bleu.*

Horas azules: *En la "Anemone Room" el baño es lo más destacado. Aquí, el huésped puede relajarse en una bañera con patas de oro. El "Pan Room", en el primer piso, se caracteriza por sus tonos dorados y las pinceladas en diferentes tonos de azul.*

L'Ora azzurra: *Nell'"Anemone Room" il bagno è l'assoluto highlight. Qui ci si rilassa in una vasca con piedi d'oro. Il "Pan Room" al primo piano vive degli accenti dorati e tocchi di colore in diverse tonalità d'azzurro.*

Four Seasons Cairo at The First Residence

Cairo, Egypt

A luxurious oasis in the middle of a hectic, loud and unbelievably fascinating Cairo—this is a good description of the hotel, located on the west bank of the Nile. A great view into the distance of the world's longest river opens up from most of the rooms in the 20-storey high hotel tower. On clear days, you can make out the pyramids on the horizon. The interiors of the 226 rooms and 43 suites are timelessly elegant with heavy, precious fabrics and carefully coordinating colors.

Einer luxuriösen Oase inmitten des hektischen, lauten und unglaublich faszinierenden Kairo gleicht das am Westufer des Nils gelegene Hotel. Von den meisten Zimmern des 20 Stockwerke hohen Hotelturms aus eröffnet sich ein weiter Blick auf den längsten Fluss der Welt. An klaren Tagen lassen sich am Horizont die Pyramiden erahnen. Die Interieurs der 226 Zimmer und 43 Suiten sind zeitlos-elegant mit schweren, kostbaren Stoffen und sorgsam aufeinander abgestimmten Farben.

Oasis de luxe au cœur de l'agitation et du bruit de cette ville du Caire incroyablement fascinante, voilà cet hôtel situé sur la rive ouest du Nil. La plupart des chambres de cet immeuble de 20 étages ont une large vue sur le fleuve le plus long du monde. Par temps clair, on aperçoit les pyramides à l'horizon. L'intérieur des 226 chambres et des 43 suites est d'une élégance intemporelle, décoré de lourdes étoffes précieuses aux couleurs soigneusement harmonisées.

Este hotel, situado en la orilla occidental del Nilo, es un lujoso oasis en medio del ajetreo y del ruido de la fascinante ciudad de El Cairo. Desde la mayoría de las habitaciones de este edificio de 20 plantas, se disfruta de una extensa vista sobre el río más largo del mundo. En los días claros es posible adivinar la silueta de las pirámides en el horizonte. Los interiores de las 226 habitaciones y 43 suites están decorados con costosos tejidos de elegancia atemporal y colores cuidadosamente combinados.

Una lussuosa oasi sembra essere l'albergo sulla riva occidentale del Nilo nel bel mezzo della febbrile e rumorosa Cairo, incredibilmente affascinante. Dalla maggior parte delle camere della torre di 20 piani si apre una larga vista sul fiume più lungo del mondo. Nei giorni sereni si ha l'impressione di vedere le piramidi all'orizzonte. All'interno le 226 camere e le 43 suites sono arredate con eleganza non soggetta alla moda, con pesanti e preziose stoffe di colori che armonizzano fra di loro scelti con cura.

Guests arriving at the hotel leave the noisy bustle of the Egyptian capital behind them.

Wer das Hotel betritt lässt das lärmende Treiben der ägyptischen Metropole hinter sich.

Quiconque pénètre dans l'hôtel laisse derrière lui le bruyant tumulte de la métropole égyptienne.

Quien entra en este hotel deja atrás el ruido y el ajetreo de la metrópoli egipcia.

Chi entra nell'albergo lascia alle sue spalle la rumorosa attività della metropoli egiziana.

Oriental splendor unfolds in the lobby, which is kept in golden tones.

Orientalische Pracht entfaltet sich in der in Goldtönen gehaltenen Lobby.

Une opulence orientale règne dans l'élégant lobby aux chaudes couleurs dorées.

La suntuosidad oriental se despliega en el vestíbulo del hotel, conservado en tonos dorados.

Lo sfarzo orientale si dispiega nella lobby, in cui dominano le tonalità dorate.

The pool bar on the roof and the elegantly designed spa compliment the comfort of the rooms and suites.

Die Poolbar auf dem Dach und der edel gestaltete Spa ergänzen den Komfort der Zimmer und Suiten.

Le bar de la piscine sur le toit et le spa élégamment aménagé complètent le confort des chambres et des suites.

El bar de la piscina en la azotea y el elegante balneario complementan el confort de las habitaciones y las suites.

Il Pool Bar sul tetto e la SPA corredata in modo eccellente completano il comfort delle camere e delle suites.

Conrad Cairo

Cairo, Egypt

When the porter with the red fez welcomes newcomers, the guests immediately feel at home. The luxury hotel in the heart of Cairo towers high above the bank of the Nile. All rooms have balconies and fantastic views of the river. In the atrium of the lobby, the marble floor shines beneath magnificent King palm trees. Four elegant restaurants, a bar decorated with traditional murals and mahogany furniture leave no doubt: The Conrad is one of the top addresses in the Middle East.

Wenn der Portier mit dem roten Fez die Neuankömmlinge empfängt, fühlen sich die Gäste gleich zu Hause. Das Luxushotel im Herzen Kairos erhebt sich hoch über dem Ufer des Nils. Alle Räume haben Balkone und phantastische Ausblicke auf den Fluss. Im Atrium der Lobby schimmert der Marmorboden unter prächtigen Königspalmen. Vier elegante Restaurants, eine mit traditioneller Malerei verzierte Bar und Mahagoni-Möbel lassen keinen Zweifel: Das Conrad ist eine der ersten Adressen im Mittleren Osten.

Quand le portier au chapeau fez rouge accueille les nouveaux arrivants, ceux-ci se sentent tout de suite chez eux. Cet hôtel de luxe au cœur du Caire s'élève bien au-dessus des rives du Nil. Toutes les chambres ont un balcon offrant une vue fantastique sur le fleuve. Dans l'atrium du lobby, le dallage de marbre brille sous les superbes palmiers royaux. Quatre restaurants, un bar orné de peintures traditionnelles et des meubles d'acajou ne laissent aucune place au doute : le Conrad est l'une des premières adresses du Moyen Orient.

Cuando el portero con el fez rojo recibe a los recién llegados, los huéspedes se sienten inmediatamente como en casa. Este lujoso hotel en el corazón de El Cairo se levanta muy por encima de la orilla del Nilo. Todas las habitaciones tienen balcones con fantásticas vistas al río. En el atrio de la entrada, los suelos de mármol refulgen bajo las palmeras reales. Cuatro elegantes restaurantes, un bar decorado con pintura tradicional y los muebles de caoba no dejan lugar a dudas: el Conrad es una de las direcciones más exclusivas en Oriente Medio.

Quando il portiere, con il fez rosso in testa, accoglie gli ospiti appena arrivati, li fa sentire subito a loro agio. L'hotel di lusso nel cuore della città del Cairo si erge in alto sulla riva del Nilo. Tutte le camere hanno balconi e vista fantastica sul fiume. Entrando nella lobby il pavimento di marmo risplende sotto magnifiche palme reali. Quattro eleganti ristoranti, un bar ornato con dipinti tradizionali e mobili in mogano non lasciano alcun dubbio: il Conrad è uno dei primi indirizzi nel Medio Oriente.

 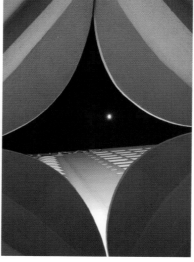

With a white façade, the hotel soars above the Nile. Visible from all rooms, the metropolis and home to millions stretches along the riverbanks.

Mit weißer Fassade ragt das Hotel über dem Nil auf. An seinen Ufern, von allen Zimmern aus sichtbar, erstreckt sich die Millionenmetropole.

Avec sa façade blanche l'hôtel se dresse au-dessus du Nil. Sur ses rives, visibles de toutes les chambres, s'étend cette métropole de plusieurs millions d'habitants.

El hotel se levanta sobre el Nilo con su fachada blanca. A orillas del río, visible desde todas las habitaciones, se extiende esta megalópolis.

Con una bianca facciata l'albergo si erge sul Nilo. Lungo le sue rive, visibili da tutte le camere, si estende la popolatissima metropoli.

Bright wall murals, paintings and sculptures of Egyptian artists decorate the restaurants, lobby and luxury suites.

Bunte Wandmalereien, Gemälde und Skulpturen ägyptischer Künstler zieren Restaurants, Lobby und Luxussuiten.

Des peintures murales multicolores, des tableaux et des sculptures d'artistes égyptiens ornent restaurants, lobby et suites de luxe.

Coloridos murales, pinturas y esculturas de artistas egipcios adornan los restaurantes, el vestíbulo y las suites de lujo.

Pitture murali in vari colori, dipinti e sculture di artisti egiziani ornano i ristoranti, gli atri e le suites di lusso.

King David Hotel

Jerusalem, Israel

Built in 1931 and named after the second king of Israel und Judea, the King David is a truly historical hotel. Famous politicians and stars were guests here and they felt like they were in an oasis in the middle of the embattled city of Jerusalem. Even today, the hotel still radiates a special aura. It is reflected in the interior and all the extras, which are to be expected of a grand hotel of this rank, including gourmet restaurant and bar. In the rooms, especially in the royal suite, guests can live like kings.

1931 erbaut und nach dem zweiten König von Israel und Juda benannt, ist das King David ein wahrhaft geschichtsträchtiges Hotel. Namhafte Politiker und Stars waren hier zu Gast und fühlten sich inmitten der umkämpften Stadt Jerusalem wie in einer Oase. Auch heute noch verströmt das Hotel eine besondere Aura. Sie spiegelt sich im Interieur und allen Extras, die ein Grand Hotel dieser Klasse erwarten lässt, Gourmetrestaurant und Bar inklusive. In den Zimmern, vor allem in der Royal Suite, lässt es sich königlich wohnen.

Construit en 1931 et portant le nom du deuxième roi d'Israël et de Judée, le King David est véritablement un hôtel porteur d'histoire. Des hommes politiques et des stars célèbres en ont été les hôtes et y ont trouvé un havre de paix au milieu de Jérusalem, cette ville convoitée. Aujourd'hui encore l'hôtel dégage une aura particulière. Celle-ci se reflète dans les intérieurs et tous les services proposés par un grand hôtel de cette catégorie, restaurant gastronomique et bar compris. Dans les chambres, en particulier dans la Suite Royale, on y vit de façon princière.

Construido en 1931 y llamado como el segundo rey de Israel y Judea, el King David es, verdaderamente, un hotel lleno de historia. Importantes políticos y famosas estrellan se han hospedado aquí, sintiéndose como en un oasis en medio de la disputada Jerusalén. Todavía hoy, el hotel emite un aura especial que se refleja en el diseño de su interior y en todos los extras que se espera de un hotel de esta categoría, como su restaurante gastronómico y su bar. En las habitaciones, especialmente en la Royal Suite, es posible sentirse como un rey.

Costruito nel 1931 il King David prende il nome dal secondo re d'Israele e Giuda ed è un Hotel pregno di storia per eccellenza. Persone conosciute del mondo politico e dello spettacolo vi hanno alloggiato e si sono sentiti come in un'oasi in mezzo alla contesa città di Gerusalemme. Ancora oggi l'albergo emana una particolare aura che si rivela negli ambienti all'interno e in tutti gli extra da aspettarsi da un Grand Hotel di questa classe, inclusi il ristorante gourmet ed il bar. Nelle camere, specialmente nella Royal Suite, si abita da re.

Five o'clock tea and strolling in the splendid gardens. Living here means much more than merely being a hotel guest.

Five o'clock tea und Lustwandeln in den herrlichen Gärten. Hier zu wohnen bedeutet weit mehr, als nur Hotelgast zu sein.

Thé de cinq heures et flânerie dans les superbes jardins. Habiter ici, c'est infiniment plus qu'être un client.

Té a las cinco en punto y agradables paseos por los maravillosos jardines. Alojarse aquí significa mucho más que ser un huésped en un hotel.

Five o'clock tea celebrare il rito inglese legato al tè e passeggiare nei meravigliosi giardini – alloggiare qui significa molto di più che essere un semplice ospite d'albergo.

The view from the windows in the upper rooms looks onto Jerusalem's old city with the golden dome of the Temple Mount.

Der Blick aus den Fenstern der oberen Räume fällt auf die Altstadt Jerusalems mit der vergoldeten Kuppel des Felsendoms.

La vue des fenêtres des étages supérieurs donne sur la vielle ville de Jérusalem avec la coupole dorée du Dôme du Rocher.

La vista desde las ventanas de las habitaciones superiores se extiende sobre el casco antiguo de la ciudad con las cúpulas doradas de la catedral de la colina.

Lo sguardo dalle finestre delle camere più in alto cade sul centro storico di Gerusalemme con la cupola dorata del Duomo della Roccia.

King David Hotel *Jerusalem, Israel* 45

Quite a few political leaders have entered this lobby with its traditional character, as well as the private dining room at La Regence Restaurant where an exclusive selection of wine can be discovered.

In den Empfang mit seinem traditionsreichen Charakter und den privaten Speiseraum im La Regence Restaurant, in dem eine Auswahl erlesener Wein zu finden ist, hat es schon manche politische Größen gezogen.

La réception au caractère porteur de traditions et la salle à manger privée du Restaurant La Regence dans laquelle se trouve une sélection de vins fins ont déjà attiré nombre d'hommes politiques éminents.

La recepción, con su carácter de larga tradición así como el comedor privado del Restaurante La Regence, con una selección de vinos escogidos, ha atraído a algunos políticos de renombre.

Dalla ricezione dell'albergo, con il suo carattere ricco di tradizioni e la sala da pranzo privata di Restaurante La Regence, dove viene offerta una scelta di vini pregiati, sono stati attirati parecchi grandi del mondo politico.

The Chedi Muscat

Muscat, Oman

On the city limits of Oman's capital Muscat lies The Chedi Muscat, a complex ensemble of white buildings that could remind the observer of the Alhambra, if it were not for the modern architecture. The courtyard waits with its intricate system of pools, a water garden lies in front of the Chedi Wing. But the facility is in no way introverted; rather all rooms offer a fascinating view, either of the nearby mountains or of the Indian Ocean. A private beach also belongs to the hotel.

Am Rande von Omans Hauptstadt Muscat liegt The Chedi Muscat, ein komplexes Ensemble strahlend weißer Gebäude, das den Betrachter an die Alhambra erinnern könnte, wäre da nicht die moderne Architektur. Die Innenhöfe warten mit einem verschlungenen System von Teichen auf, vor dem Chedi Wing liegt ein Wassergarten. Doch die Anlage ist keineswegs introvertiert, vielmehr bieten alle Zimmer eine faszinierende Aussicht, entweder auf die nahe gelegenen Berge oder auf den Indischen Ozean. Ein Privatstrand gehört ebenfalls zum Hotel.

A la périphérie de Muscat, la capitale d'Oman, se situe le Chedi Muscat, un ensemble complexe de bâtiments d'un blanc rayonnant qui rappelle au visiteur l'Alhambra, sans parler du caractère moderne de l'architecture. Les cours intérieures offrent un système complexe et sinueux de bassins ; devant le Chedi Wing se trouve un jardin d'eau. Cependant, le domaine n'est pas du tout replié sur lui-même ; toutes les fenêtres offrent une vue fascinante soit sur les montagnes voisines, soit sur l'océan Indien. L'hôtel possède également une plage privée.

Al borde de la capital de Omán, Muscat, está ubicado The Chedi Muscat, un conjunto de construcciones de radiante blancura que podría traer a la memoria del observador el palacio de la Alhambra, si no fuera por la arquitectura moderna. Los patios interiores presentan un complejo sistema de estanques y delante del Chedi Wing se encuentra un jardín acuático. No obstante, el resort no está en absoluto encerrado en sí mismo; todas las habitaciones ofrecen una vista fascinante de las montañas cercanas o del Océano Indico. El hotel también cuenta con una playa privada.

Ai bordi della capitale dell'Oman Muscat si trova The Chedi Muscat, un insieme complesso d'edifici bianchi splendenti che all'ospite potrebbe ricordare l'Alhambra, se non fosse per l'architettura moderna. I cortili interni si presentano con un sistema intrecciato di stagni, davanti al Chedi Wing si trova un giardino d'acqua. L'impianto tuttavia non è introverso, poiché tutte le camere offrono un panorama affascinante sulle vicine montagne oppure sull'Oceano Indiano. Una spiaggia privata fa altresì parte dell'hotel.

Whether it's a sea view or relaxing indoors—The Chedi Muscat opens the door on a world of the extraordinary. A clear form language defines the design in the suites and rooms.

Ob Meerblick oder Entspannung im Inneren—The Chedi Muscat öffnet das Tor zu einer Welt des Außergewöhnlichen. In den Suiten und Zimmern bestimmt eine klare Formensprache das Design.

Que ce soit la vue sur la mer ou la détente à l'intérieur, le Chedi Muscat ouvre la porte d'un monde exceptionnel. Dans les suites et les chambres, la conception est marquée par des formes épurées.

Vistas al mar y relajación en su interior, The Chedi Muscat abre las puertas a un mundo excepcional. En las suites y habitaciones, un lenguaje formal sencillo determina el diseño.

Vista sul mare o rilassarsi all'interno dell'edificio—The Chedi Muscat apre le porte ad un mondo fuori del comune. Nelle suites e nelle camere il design viene definito da una chiara espressione delle forme.

The hotel's cosmopolitan character is influenced by the successful combination of east and west.

Es ist die gelungene Verbindung von Orient und Okzident, die den kosmopolitischen Charakter des Hotels kennzeichnet.

C'est l'association réussie de l'Orient et de l'Occident qui caractérise le caractère cosmopolite de cet hôtel.

El cosmopolita carácter del hotel surge de la lograda unión entre Oriente y Occidente.

È la ben riuscita unione fra l'oriente e l'occidente che dà tono al carattere cosmopolita dell'albergo.

The Chedi Muscat *is still one of the few examples which show oriental minimalism.*

Das Chedi Muscat *ist eines der noch seltenen Beispiele für orientalischen Minimalismus.*

Le Chedi Muscat *est toujours un des rares exemples qui montrent le minimalisme oriental.*

El Chedi Muscat *sigue siendo uno de los pocos ejemplos que muestra minimalismo oriental.*

Il Chedi Muscat *è ancora uno dei pochi esempi che mostrano il minimalismo orientale.*

Emirates Palace Abu Dhabi

Abu Dhabi, United Arab Emirates

Like a palace out of Thousand and One Nights—this is how Abu Dhabi's newest and top-class luxury hotel looks. Located in the middle of an 80-hectare park landscape, the two wings of the building measure one kilometer in length. 114 domes define its silhouette. The majestic oriental luxury of the interior is matched by the gigantic exterior appearance. Even the technical equipment sets standards: in the 394 rooms and suites, there are 755 plasma screens.

Wie ein Palast aus Tausendundeiner Nacht mutet Abu Dhabis neuestes Luxushotel der Superlative an. Inmitten einer 80 Hektar großen Parklandschaft gelegen, misst das Gebäude mit seinen zwei Flügeln einen Kilometer in der Länge. 114 Kuppeln bestimmen seine Silhouette. Der gigantischen äußeren Erscheinung entspricht der prunkvolle orientalische Luxus des Interieurs. Selbst die technische Ausstattung setzt Maßstäbe: Allein 755 Plasma-Bildschirme befinden sich in den 394 Zimmer und Suiten.

Tel un palais des Mille et Une Nuits ce nouvel établissement d'un luxe extrême est à Abou Dhabi. Situé au cœur d'un immense parc de 80 hectares, le bâtiment constitué de deux ailes mesure un kilomètre de long. Sa silhouette est marquée par 114 coupoles. Les fastes orientaux des intérieurs sont à l'égal de cette apparition gigantesque. Les équipements technologiques mêmes sont une première : 755 écrans plasma viennent équiper les 394 chambres et suites.

Como un palacio sacado de las Mil y una noches, el Abu Dhabis, el último hotel de lujo construido, alcanza el grado de superlativo. En medio de un parque de 80 hectáreas, el edificio junto con sus dos alas llega al kilómetro de longitud. 114 cúpulas conforman su contorno. Su gigantesca apariencia exterior refleja el suntuoso lujo oriental de su interior. Incluso su equipamiento tecnológico establece nuevas pautas: un total de 755 pantallas de plasma se reparten entre sus 394 habitaciones y suites.

Come un palazzo da Mille e una notte si presenta l'albergo di lusso dei superlativi costruito di recente. In un parco il cui paesaggio si estende per ben 80 ettari, l'edificio con le sue due ali è lungo un chilometro. La sua silhouette è formata da 114 cupole. Al gigantesco aspetto esterno corrisponde il lusso sfarzoso orientale all'interno. Persino le attrezzature tecniche fissano criteri: ben 755 schermi al plasma, per esempio, sono posizionati nelle 394 camere e nelle suites.

On the 1.3 kilometer stretch of beach: Abu Dhabi's newest landmark is situated here.

Am 1,3 Kilometer langen Sandstrand liegt Abu Dhabis neuestes Wahrzeichen.

Au bord d'1,3 kilomètre de plage de sable s'étend le nouvel emblème d'Abou Dhabi.

En una playa de 1,3 kilómetros se encuentra el nuevo símbolo de Abu Dhabis.

Lungo la spiaggia che si estende per 1,3 chilometri è ubicato il nuovo simbolo di Abu Dhabis

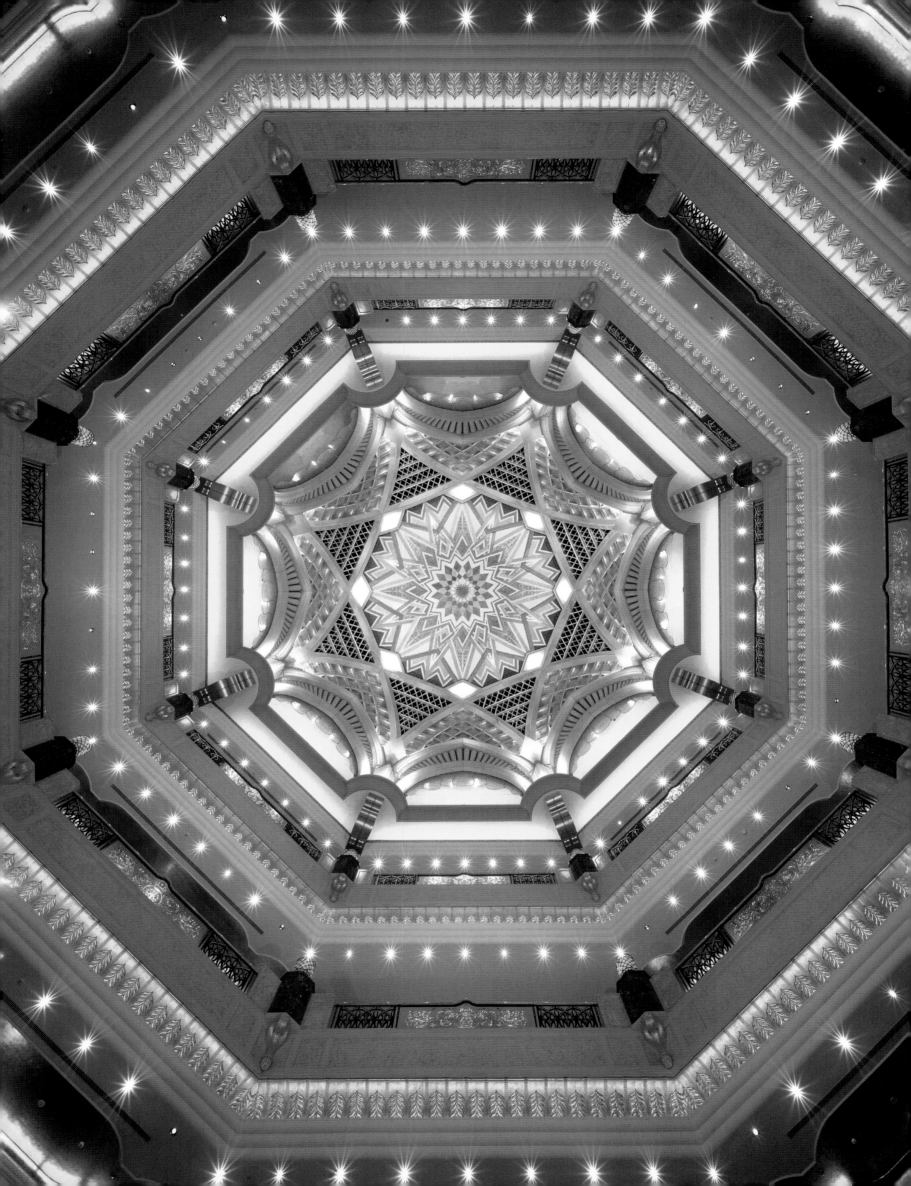

Precious mosaics in traditional Arabian ornamentation decorate the great domes of the atrium and the lobby.

Kostbare Mosaiken in traditioneller arabischer Ornamentik schmücken die großen Kuppeln des Atriums und der Lobby.

Des précieuses mosaïques dans la tradition ornementale arabe décorent les grandes coupoles de l'atrium et du lobby.

Costosos mosaicos dentro de la tradicional ornamentación árabe, adornan las grandes cúpulas del atrio y el vestíbulo.

Preziosi mosaici abbelliscono nel modo tradizionale dell'arte araba le grandi cupole dell'atrio e della lobby.

Emirates Palace Abu Dhabi *Abu Dhabi, United Arab Emirates* 57

More than 1,000 chandeliers, decorated with valuable Swarovski crystals, are to be found throughout the hotel.

Mehr als 1.000 Lüster, bestückt mit wertvollen Swarovski-Kristallen, finden sich im gesamten Hotel.

Plus de 1 000 lustres avec de précieux cristaux Swarovski illuminent l'ensemble de l'hôtel.

En el hotel cuelgan más de 1000 lámparas de araña adornadas con cristal Swarovski.

Píu di 1000 lampadari, corredati di preziosi cristalli Swarovski, si trovano in il entero albergo.

Beit al Bahar Villas

Dubai, United Arab Emirates

"House by the Sea"—the translation of the Arabian name provides the clue for the favored location of the 19 villas on the fine-grained, white sandy beach in view of Dubai's striking landmark, the Burj al Arab. The ochre colored villas built of clay are grouped around a pool. High clay walls shelter small private gardens. The building style is inspired by the Arabian legacy of the desert state. Thick Persian rugs and luxuriously embroidered silk cushions emphasize the oriental atmosphere.

„Haus am Meer" – die Übersetzung des arabischen Namens liefert den Hinweis auf die bevorzugte Lage der 19 Villen am feinkörnigen weißen Sandstrand in Sichtweite des Aufsehen erregenden Wahrzeichens Dubais, des Burj al Arab. Die ockerfarbenen, aus Lehm gebauten Villen gruppieren sich um einen Pool. Hohe Lehmmauern schirmen kleine Privatgärten ab. Die Bauweise orientiert sich am arabischen Erbe des Wüstenstaats. Dicke Perserteppiche und prächtig bestickte Seidenkissen unterstreichen das orientalische Ambiente.

« Maison au bord de la mer » – la traduction du nom arabe explique bien l'emplacement privilégié des 19 villas au bord d'une plage de sable fin et blanc à proximité du Burj al Arab, le sensationnel emblème de Dubaï. Les villas d'argile aux couleurs ocre sont groupées autour d'une piscine. De hauts murs d'argile protègent de petits jardins privés. L'architecture met en œuvre l'héritage arabe de cet état du désert. D'épais tapis persans et des coussins de soie admirablement brodés soulignent l'atmosphère orientale.

"Casa en el mar", la traducción del nombre árabe apunta ya hacia la ubicación escogida para estas 19 villas, una playa de arena blanca y fina desde la que es posible ver el espectacular símbolo de Dubai, el Burj al Arab. Estas villas de color ocre y construidas de barro, se levantan en torno a una piscina. Los altos muros de adobe protegen los pequeños jardines privados. El estilo arquitectónico se inspira en la herencia árabe del estado desértico. Las gruesas alfombras persas y los cojines ricamente bordados acentúan el ambiente oriental.

"Casa al mare" – la traduzione del nome arabo indica la posizione privilegiata delle 19 ville lungo la spiaggia dalla sabbia bianca e fine, non lontana dal sensazionale simbolo di Dubai, il Burj Al Arab. Le ville costruite in argilla di color ocra si raggruppano intorno a una piscina. Alte mura d'argilla fanno da schermo a piccoli giardini privati. Il genere di costruzione è orientato al patrimonio culturale arabo di questo Stato nel deserto. Spessi tappeti persiani e cuscini in seta sfarzosamente ricamati sottolineano l'ambiente orientale.

Sheltered by high walls, guests can relax in the shade of the sister hotel Burj al Arab.

Geschützt von hohen Mauern können die Gäste im Schatten des Schwesterhotels Burj al Arab relaxen.

Protégés par de hauts murs, les hôtes peuvent se détendre à l'ombre du Burj al Arab.

Protegidos por los altos muros, los huéspedes pueden relajarse a la sombra del hotel vecino, el Burj al Arab.

Protetti da alte mura gli ospiti possono rilassarsi all'ombra dell'albergo gemello Burj al Arab.

In the interior of the villas, dark wood, decorated with intricate ornaments and heavy fabrics in Bordeaux and gold tones are predominant.

Im Inneren der Villen dominieren dunkles, mit aufwendigen Ornamenten verziertes Holz und schwere Stoffe in Bordeaux- und Goldtönen.

L'intérieur des villas est caractérisé par du bois sombre garni de riches ornements et de lourdes étoffes dans des tons bordeaux et or.

En el interior de las villas dominan la madera, oscura y muy trabajada, y los paños pesados, en tonos burdeos y dorados.

All'interno delle ville sono dominanti il legno decorato con costosi ornamenti e pesanti stoffe in tonalità dorate e in bordeaux.

One&Only Royal Mirage

Dubai, United Arab Emirates

Domes made from clay slates, low walls and date palms swaying in the wind define the silhouette of the luxury hotel village on the blinding white Jumeirah beach, which strictly speaking consists of three different resorts. A fountain in the inner courtyard, around which generous divans are positioned, emphasizes the Arabian appearance. The Givenchy spa, a traditional hammam and the pool landscape, sheltered by palms, offer perfect relaxation.

Kuppeln aus Lehmziegeln, niedrige Mauern und sich im Wind wiegende Dattelpalmen bestimmen die Silhouette des luxuriösen Hoteldorfs am blenden weißen Jumeirah Beach, das genau genommen aus drei unterschiedlichen Resorts besteht. Ein Brunnen im Innenhof, um den sich ausladende Diwane gruppieren, unterstreicht die arabische Anmutung. Der Givenchy-Spa, ein traditionelles Hammam und die von Palmen beschattete Poollandschaft bieten perfekte Entspannung.

Des coupoles de tuiles en argile, des murets et des dattiers se balançant au vent dessinent la silhouette de ce complexe hôtelier luxueux au bord de la plage de Jumeirah d'un blanc éblouissant composé en fait de trois resorts distincts. L'atmosphère arabe est soulignée par une fontaine au milieu du patio autour duquel se trouvent des divans invitant au repos. Le Spa Givenchy, un hammam traditionnel et la piscine ombragée de palmiers assurent une parfaite détente.

Las cúpulas de ladrillo de adobe, los muros bajos y las palmeras de dátiles cimbreadas por el viento, forman la línea del contorno de este lujoso pueblo hotel compuesto, en realidad, por tres centros levantados en la luminosa playa blanca Jumeirah Beach. La fuente, situada en el centro del patio interior y rodeada de amplios divanes, subraya el acento árabe. El balneario Givenchy, un hamman tradicional y la piscina rodeada de palmeras, ofrecen el escenario perfecto para la relajación.

Cupole in mattoni d'argilla, basse mura e palme da datteri ondeggianti al vento caratterizzano la silhouette del lussuosissimo impianto residenziale al Jumeirah Beach di un biancore splendente e composto di tre strutture. Una fontana nel cortile interno, attorno alla quale si raggruppano ampi e invitanti divani, accentua la grazia arabica. La Givencchy-SPA, un Hammam tradizionale e il susseguirsi di piscine ombreggiate da palme offrono puro relax.

Elegant opulence influences the dining room of the Residence & Spa, which is flooded in light.

Elegante Opulenz prägen den Licht durchfluteten Speisesaal des Residence & Spa.

Une élégante opulence caractérise la salle à manger inondée de lumière de la Résidence & Spa.

La elegancia y la opulencia caracterizan el comedor bañado en luz del Residence&Spa.

Una ricercata opulenza dà una nota particolare alla sala da pranzo del Residence & SPA inondata di luce.

On the terrace of the Samovar Lounge even the shade has an Arabian pattern in the afternoons. In the suites, the baths are the size of what are normally living rooms.

Auf der Terrasse der Samovar Lounge hat nachmittags sogar der Schatten ein arabisches Muster. In den Suiten haben die Bäder Ausmaße wie sonst nur Wohnzimmmer.

Sur la terrasse de la Samovar Lounge, l'après-midi, même l'ombre forme des motifs arabes. Dans les suites, les salles de bains sont aussi spacieuses qu'ordinairement les salles de séjour.

Incluso la sombra tiene un dibujo árabe al caer la tarde en la terraza del salón Samovar. En las suites, las medidas de los baños son similares a las de un cuarto de estar.

Sulla terrazza del Samovar Lounge di pomeriggio persino l'ombra è fatta di ornamenti arabi. Nelle suites i bagni hanno dimensioni da camere di soggiorno.

Madinat Jumeirah
Dubai, United Arab Emirates

Waterways meander through the Madinat, built like a traditional Arabian village, with the three hotels Mina A'Salam, Al Quasr, Dar Al Masyaf and its cheery and colorful souk. The Jumeirah group's hotel village stretches for almost four kilometers by the sea. Guests can reach the 44 different restaurants and bars by wooden water taxis. Or they can visit the Six Senses Spa, with its 30 freestanding treatment rooms, surrounded by luscious and blooming gardens and one of the largest fitness zones in the Middle East.

Wasserwege mäandern durch das wie ein traditionelles arabisches Dorf gebaute Madinat mit den drei Hotels Mina A'Salam, Al Quasr, Dar Al Masyaf und seinem farbenfrohen Suk. Fast vier Kilometer zieht sich das Hoteldorf der Jumeirah Gruppe am Meer entlang. Gäste können mit Wassertaxis aus Holz die 44 verschiedenen Restaurants und Bars erreichen. Oder das Six Senses Spa, der mit seinen 30 freistehenden Behandlungsräumen, umgeben von üppig blühenden Gärten, als der größte Wellnessbereich im Mittleren Osten gilt.

Des canaux artificiels sillonnent le Madinat, ensemble construit comme un village arabe traditionnel et comprenant les trois hôtels Mina A'Salam, Al Quasr, Dar Al Masyaf ainsi que son souk bariolé. Le complexe hôtelier de la chaîne Jumeirah s'étire sur presque quatre kilomètres le long de la mer. Les hôtes sont emmenés par bateau en bois aux 44 différents restaurants et bars. Ou au Six Senses Spa, le centre de fitness considéré comme le plus grand du Moyen Orient avec ses 30 salles de soins autonomes, entouré de jardins fleuris luxuriants.

Las acequias, que discurren formando meandros, atraviesan el Madinat, una instalación construida imitando un pueblo árabe y compuesta por tres hoteles, Mina A'Salam, Al Quasr y Dar Al Masyaf, y un colorido *suk* o plaza del mercado. Este pueblo hotel del grupo Jumeirah se extiende a lo largo de la costa durante casi cuatro kilómetros. Los huéspedes pueden dirigirse a los 44 restaurantes y bares a bordo de taxis de madera. O pueden visitar el Six Senses Spa que, con sus 30 zonas independientes de tratamiento rodeadas de exuberantes jardines, está considerado como el centro de salud y bienestar más grande del Oriente Medio.

Vie d'acqua formano meandri attraverso il Madinat, costruito come un paese tradizionale arabo, con i tre alberghi Mina A'Salam, Al Qasr, Dar Al Masyaf ed il suo souk dai colori vivaci. La struttura del gruppo Jumeirah si estende lungo il mare per quasi quattro chilometri. Gli ospiti possono raggiungere con piccole imbarcazioni-taxi di legno i 44 diversi ristoranti e bar oppure farsi portare alla Six Senses SPA, che con i suoi 30 locali per i vari trattamenti, a sé stanti e circondati da giardini lussureggianti, è considerato il più grande centro benessere del Medio Oriente.

Although architecture and interiors are also richly embellished here, the hotel complex and rooms do not appear overloaded. The reason for the optical serenity is primarily the harmonious color scheme.

Obwohl Architektur und Interieur auch hier reich ornamentiert sind, wirken die Anlage und die Zimmer nicht überladen. Der Grund für die optische Ruhe ist in erster Linie eine harmonische Farbgebung.

Bien que l'architecture et l'intérieur soient ici richement ornementés, le complexe et les chambres ne donnent pas une impression de surcharge. En effet, un choix de couleurs harmonieux leur confère cette tranquillité visuelle.

A pesar de la rica ornamentación de la arquitectura y de los interiores, las instalaciones y las habitaciones no transmiten la sensación de estar recargadas. La tranquilidad óptica se consigue gracias a la armonía de los colores.

Nonostante l'architettura e gli ambienti all'interno siano anche qui ricchi di ornamenti, l'impianto residenziale e le camere non danno l'impressione di essere sovraccariche. La ragione per cui l'occhio possa godere di una benefica e gradevole calma è da cercare nella sapiente e armoniosa disposizione dei colori.

A delightful contrast: the view over the hotel village with its waterways to Dubai's spectacular landmark, the Burj al Arab or Jumeirah International.

Ein reizvoller Kontrast: Der Blick über das Hoteldorf mit seinen Wasserwegen auf das spektakuläre Wahrzeichen Dubais, das Burj al Arab.

Un contraste plein de charme: la vue au-dessus du complexe hôtelier avec son réseau de canaux sur le spectaculaire emblème de Dubai, le Burj al Arab.

Un contraste encantador: la vista sobre el pueblo hotel y sus acequias con el espectacular símbolo de Dubai, el Burj al Arab, al fondo.

Un'affascinante contrasto: La vista al di sopra dell'impianto residenziale con le sue vie d'acqua sullo spettacolare Burj al Arab, che con la sua forma di vela spiegata è diventato il simbolo di Dubai.

The interior design is—how could it be otherwise—inspired by the palatial style, with lots of marble and carvings. The Six Senses Spa, on the other hand, appears stark and modern.

Die Innenraumgestaltung ist – wie könnte es anders sein – einem Palast nachempfunden, mit viel Marmor und Schnitzarbeiten. Sachlich modern gibt sich dagegen das Six Senses Spa.

La réalisation des intérieurs ressemble – comment pourrait-il en être autrement – à celle d'un palais, avec beaucoup de marbre et de sculptures sur bois. Le Six Senses Spa est, quant à lui, résolument moderne et fonctionnel.

El diseño interior del espacio está inspirado, como no, en el de un palacio, con abundancia de mármol y tallas de madera. En contraste, el Six Senses Spa ha sido concebido en una línea más moderna.

L'arredamento all'interno è – ovviamente – adeguato ad un palazzo, con tanto marmo e lavori d'intaglio. Razionale e moderno si presenta invece il centro benessere Six Senses SPA.

Jumeirah Bab Al Shams

Dubai, United Arab Emirates

"Gateway to the Sun" is the promising Arabian name of the newest highlight of the Jumeirah group, which seduces its guests with the atmosphere of an Arabian oasis city. The desert resort, located 35 minutes by car from Dubai-city, consists of 16 two-storey buildings, which are connected to each other by inner courtyards and serpentine stone stairways. In the Satori Spa, Arabian-inspired treatments are on offer.

„Tor zur Sonne" lautet der viel versprechende arabische Name des neuesten Highlights der Jumeirah-Gruppe, das seine Gäste in die Atmosphäre einer arabischen Oasenstadt entführt. Das 35 Autominuten von Dubai-Stadt entfernte Wüstenresort besteht aus 16 zweistöckigen Gebäuden, die durch Innenhöfe und gewundene Steintreppen miteinander verbunden sind. Im Satori-Spa werden arabisch inspirierte Behandlungen angeboten.

« Porte du soleil », tel est le nom arabe très prometteur du tout dernier événement de la chaîne Jumeirah qui transporte ses hôtes dans l'atmosphère d'une oasis arabe. Cet hôtel au cœur du désert, à 35 minutes de la ville de Dubai, se compose de 16 bâtiments à deux étages reliés entre eux par des cours intérieures et de tortueux escaliers de pierre. Le Satori-Spa propose des soins d'inspiration arabe.

"La puerta al sol", esta es la traducción del árabe del prometedor nombre del nuevo hotel del grupo Jumeirah. Con él se pretende trasladar a los huéspedes al ambiente de una ciudad oasis árabe. A 35 minutos en coche de Dubai, esta instalación hotelera levantada en el desierto está compuesta por edificios de 16 plantas, unidos entre sí por patios interiores y sinuosas escaleras de piedra. En el balneario Satori se ofrecen tratamientos de tradición árabe.

"Porta che conduce al sole" è il nome arabo molto promettente dell'ultimo highlight del gruppo Jumeirah, che trasporta i suoi ospiti nell'atmosfera di un'oasi araba. Il resort nel deserto dista dalla città di Dubai 35 minuti di macchina e consiste in 16 edifici a due piani, collegati fra di loro tramite cortili interni e scale in pietra a chiocciola. Nella Satori-SPA vengono offerti trattamenti ispirati alle usanze arabe sul campo.

The dark handcrafted wooden furniture and kilims that decorate the 105 rooms and ten suites in restrained style perfectly correspond to the exterior of the buildings.

Die mit dunklen handgefertigten Holzmöbeln und Kelims zurückhaltend dekorierten 105 Zimmer und zehn Suiten korrespondieren perfekt mit dem Äußeren der Gebäude.

Les 105 chambres et les dix suites, discrètement décorées de meubles sombres fabriqués par des artisans et de kelims, sont en parfaite harmonie avec l'aspect extérieur des bâtiments.

La discreta decoración de las 105 habitaciones, con muebles oscuros de madera hechos a mano y alfombras kelim, se corresponde perfectamente con el aspecto exterior de los edificios.

Gli scuri mobili in legno fatti a mano ed i Kilim che decorano con discrezione le 105 camere e le dieci suites sono in perfetta armonia con l'esterno dell'edificio.

Clay rendering on the masonry and the soft light of lanterns inspire a desert feel.

Lehm verputztes Mauerwerk und sanftes Laternenlicht vermitteln Wüsten-Feeling.

Des murs au crépi d'argile et la douce lumière des lanternes recréent l'atmosphère du désert.

Los muros de mampostería y la suave luz de las farolas transmiten al huésped la sensación de encontrarse en el desierto.

Le mura con l'intonaco in argilla e la luce calma e gradevole delle lanterne infondono il giusto feeling a contatto col deserto.

From the pool deck, a fantastic view opens up over the desert landscape.

Vom Pooldeck eröffnet sich ein grandioser Blick in die Wüstenlandschaft.

Du bord de la piscine s'ouvre un panorama grandiose sur les paysages du désert.

Desde la piscina se extiende una grandiosa vista sobre el desierto.

Dal bordo piscina si apre una grandiosa vista sul paesaggio del deserto.

Al Maha Desert Resort & Spa

Dubai, United Arab Emirates

Close to the sky and closer to heaven is the sensation that guests at this unique resort are given, located in the seemingly endless expanse of the Arabian desert, yet only 45 minutes from Dubai. At night, a blanket of stars spans above the hotel's 40 suites, built in the style of a village of Bedouin tents. During the day, guests can observe the protected Oryx gazelles from their terraces—the creature that lends it's Arabic name, Al Maha, to the resort—or be pampered at the Jamilah Spa with traditional Arabian treatments.

Dem Himmel ganz nah können sich die Gäste dieses einzigartigen Resorts fühlen, das nur 45 Autominuten von Dubai entfernt mitten in der unendlich scheinenden Weite der arabischen Wüste liegt. Nächtens spannt sich ein klarer Sternenhimmel über die im Stil eines Beduinenzeltdorfes gebauten 40 Hotel-Suiten. Tagsüber kann man von seiner Terrasse aus die bedrohten Onyx-Gazellen (arabisch: Al Maha) beobachten, die als Namenspaten fungieren, oder sich im Jumilah Spa mit überlieferten arabischen Anwendungen verwöhnen lassen.

Proches du ciel, c'est ce qu'éprouveront les hôtes de ce resort unique situé à 45 minutes de Dubai au milieu des étendues presque infinies du désert arabe. La nuit, les 40 suites de ce village de tentes bédouin ont un ciel étoilé pour toile de fond. Le jour, on peut observer de sa terrasse les gazelles Onyx (en arabe Al Maha), ici protégées, auxquelles l'hôtel doit son nom ou profiter des traitements arabes ancestraux dans le Jumilah Spa.

Los huéspedes de esta exclusiva instalación hotelera pueden sentirse muy cerca del cielo. Situado a sólo 45 minutos en coche de Dubai, el hotel se encuentra en medio del infinito paisaje del desierto árabe. Por la noche, el claro cielo cubierto de estrellas se despliega sobre las 40 suites del hotel, que evocan un pueblo de tiendas beduinas. Durane el día es posible observar a las amenazadas gacelas Onyx, cuyo nombre en árabe, Al Maha, ha dado nombre también a este hotel. El visitante también puede relajarse en el balneario Jumilah, donde se ofrecen tratamientos árabes.

Vicinissimi al cielo si possono sentire gli ospiti di questo straordinario resort, che dista solo 45 minuti di macchina da Dubai, ubicato in mezzo al deserto arabo, che sembra estendersi all'infinito. Di notte si stende un cielo chiaro e stellato sulle 40 suites — struttura ispirata agli accampamenti beduini. Di giorno si possono osservare dalla propria terrazza le gazzelle del deserto, Onyx (in arabo: Al Maha), minacciate d'estinzione, che fungono da padrini del nome, o abbandonarsi alle cure del centro benessere Jumilah SPA con i suoi antichi trattamenti tradizionali tramandati.

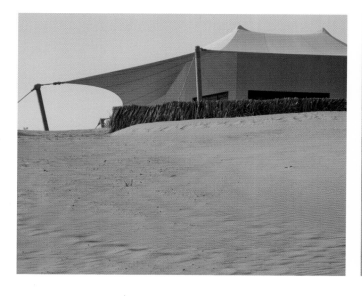 

Architecture and colors reflect the cultural heritage of the desert.

Architektur und Farben spiegeln das kulturelle Erbe der Wüste wieder.

L'architecture et les couleurs sont le reflet de l'héritage culturel du désert.

La arquitectura y los colores reflejan la herencia cultural del desierto.

Architettura e colori rispecchiano il retaggio culturale del deserto.

All funiture in the suites, which offer at least 75 m² of space, was created from finest mahogany by local craftsmen.

Sämtliche Möbel der mindestens 75 m² großen Suiten wurden von einheimischen Handwerkern aus edlem Mahagoni gefertigt.

La totalité des meubles d'acajou des suites d'au moins 75 m² a été fabriquée par des artisans autochtones.

Todos los muebles de las suites, de 75 m² como mínimo, han sido elaborados por artesanos nativos a partir de madera de caoba.

Tutti i mobili delle suites, grandi non meno di 75 m², sono stati fatti da artigiani del luogo in mogano di alto valore.

The spacious terraces offer a spectacular view of the Hajar Mountains.

Von den weitläufigen Terrassen bietet sich ein spektakulärer Blick auf das Hajar Gebirge.

Des vastes terrasses on découvre une vue époustouflante sur le massif du Hajar.

Desde las amplias terrazas se puede disfrutar de una espectacular vista sobre las montañas Hajar.

Dalle ampie e spaziose terrazze si offre allo sguardo una spettacolare vista sulla catena montuosa dell'Hajar.

84   Al Maha Desert Resort & Spa *Dubai, United Arab Emirates*

Frégate Island Private

Frégate Island, Seychelles

Close to the equator, the tiny island lies in the Indian Ocean. Powdery sand on seven beaches surrounds this resort. It has a sensitive ecosystem with rare animal species such as the Frigate bird, famous for its two-meter wingspan and after which the island was named. In the past, it incidentally served as a pirate's hideout and the buccaneers seem to have left their treasures in the villas' living and bedrooms: African hand carved beds, Javanese sculptures, Egyptian cotton.

Nur wenige Grade vom Äquator entfernt liegt die winzige Insel im Indischen Ozean. Puderiger Sand an sieben Stränden umgibt dieses Resort. Es besitzt ein sensibles Ökosystem mit seltenen Tierarten wie dem Frégate-Vogel, der berühmt ist für seine zwei Meter Flügelspannweite und nach dem die Insel benannt ist. Früher diente sie übrigens als Piratenversteck und es scheint so, als hätten die Seeräuber in den Wohn- und Schlafzimmern der Villen ihre Schätze zurückgelassen: Handgeschnitzte Betten aus Afrika, Skulpturen aus Java, Baumwolle aus Ägypten.

A seulement quelques degrés de l'équateur, cette île minuscule se trouve dans l'océan indien. Sept plages au sable fin comme de la poudre entourent ce domaine. Celui-ci possède un écosystème sensible accueillant des espèces animales rares telles que la frégate, oiseau célèbre pour les deux mètres d'envergure de ses ailes et qui donne son nom à l'île. Celle-ci servait autrefois de cachette aux pirates; et il se pourrait qu'ils aient laissé leurs trésors dans les chambres et les salons des villas : des lits sculptés à la main originaires d'Afrique, des sculptures de Java, du coton d'Egypte.

A pocos grados de latitud de la línea ecuatorial, se encuentra esta pequeña isla en el Océano Índico. El resort está rodeado de siete playas de fina arena. Posee un ecosistema muy sensible con especies animales raras, como el pájaro fragata, famoso por la envergadura de dos metros de sus alas y del cual la isla adoptó el nombre. Por cierto, ésta sirvió de escondite de piratas y todo parece indicar que éstos hubiesen dejado sus tesoros en las salas y los dormitorios de los chalés: Camas africanas talladas a mano, esculturas de Java, algodón de Egipto.

La minuscola isola si trova a soli pochi gradi dall'Equatore nell'Oceano Indiano. Sabbia fine come la polvere su sette spiagge circonda questo resort. Dispone di un sensibile ecosistema con specie rari di animali come l'uccello frégate che è famoso per la sua apertura alare di due metri e secondo il quale l'isola porta il nome. In tempi passati l'isola serviva da nascondiglio per pirati e sembra che i pirati abbiano lasciato i loro tesori nei soggiorni e le camere da letto delle ville: letti intagliati a mano dall'Africa, sculture dal Java, cotone dall'Egitto.

The newest addition is "The Rock Spa" at one of the island's highest points. From the "Infinity Pool", which is also new, guests have a panoramic view of the Indian Ocean.

Die neueste Ergänzung ist „The Rock Spa" auf einem der höchstgelegenen Stellen der Insel. Vom ebenso neuen „Infinity Pool" hat man einen Panoramablick auf den Indischen Ozean.

Le complément le plus récent est « The Rock Spa » bâti sur l'un des points les plus élevés de l'île. De la toute récente piscine « Infinity », on a une vue panoramique sur l'océan indien.

El último complemento añadido ha sido "The Rock Spa" situado en un lugar elevado de la isla. La piscina "Infinity" es también una novedad y desde ella se disfruta de una vista panorámica sobre el Océano Índico.

Recentemente si è aggiunto "The Rock Spa", ubicato su una delle maggiori alture dell'isola. Dalla piscina, "l'Infinity Pool", nuova anch'essa, si ha vista panoramica sull'oceano indiano.

40 guests share seven private beaches. But this only happens when all 16 villas are occupied. Every home has a jacuzzi with a private pavilion.

40 Gäste teilen sich sieben private Strände. Und das auch nur dann, wenn alle 16 Villen voll belegt sind. Jedes Domizil hat ein Whirlpool mit eigenem Pavillon.

40 hôtes se partagent sept plages privées. Mais ceci, seulement quand les 16 villas affichent complet. Chacune d'entre elles dispose d'un jacuzzi avec pavillon individuel.

40 huéspedes comparten siete playas privadas, pero sólo si las 16 villas están completamente ocupadas. Cada casa dispone de una piscina de hidromasaje con un pabellón particular.

40 ospiti si dividono sette spiagge private, ma solo quando tutte e 16 le ville sono occupate al completo. Ogni domicilio ha un Whirlpool a cui appartiene con un suo padiglione.

An exquisite cuisine is served to guests in their villas or in the central restaurant. The bar is situated high above the ocean in the style of a pirate's hideaway.

Eine exquisite Küche versorgt die Gäste in ihren Villen oder im zentralen Restaurant. Im Stil eines Seeräuberverstecks ist die hoch über dem Ozean liegende Bar gestaltet.

Une exquise cuisine est servie aux hôtes soit dans leur villa soit dans le restaurant central. Le bar en plein air surplombant l'océan simule un repère de pirates.

Una cocina exquisita sirve a los huéspedes en sus propias villas o en el restaurante central. El diseño del bar, situado a gran altura sobre el océano, está inspirado en los escondites de piratas.

Un'eccellente cucina ristora gli ospiti nelle loro ville o nel ristorante centrale. Il bar, posto in alto con vista sull'oceano, è tenuto in stile eremo corsaro.

North Island Lodge

North Island, Seychelles

A unique symbiosis of ecology and intelligent luxury has been achieved on the isle, which measures nearly 750 hectares and is 32 kilometers northwest of Mahé. The ecological clock is supposed to be turned back again and the island wilderness, uninhabited for years, is to be recultivated. Eleven, 450 m² villas, with every imaginable luxury, provide space for a maximum of 22 guests, who observe the ambitious project and at the same time can also enjoy feeling a little like Robinson himself. This is an experience, which can become addictive, and at the very least makes a lasting impression and inspires.

Eine einzigartige Symbiose aus Ökologie und intelligentem Luxus ist auf dem knapp 750 Hektar großen Eiland 32 Kilometer nordwestlich von Mahé gelungen. Die ökologische Uhr soll wieder zurückgedreht, die jahrelang unbewohnte, verwilderte Insel rekultiviert werden. Elf 450 m² große, über allen erdenklichen Komfort verfügende Villen bieten Platz für maximal 22 Gäste, die das ehrgeizige Projekt beobachten und sich dabei ein wenig wie Robinson fühlen können. Ein Erlebnis, das süchtig machen kann, zumindest aber nachhaltig berührt und inspiriert.

Une extraordinaire réussite, la symbiose entre écologie et luxe intelligent sur cette île d'environ 750 hectares à 32 kilomètres au nord ouest de Mahé. L'objectif est de remonter aux sources de l'écologie et de recultiver cette île longtemps inhabitée et laissée à l'abandon. Onze villas de 450 m² possédant tout le confort possible hébergent un maximum de 22 hôtes qui observent cet ambitieux projet et peuvent se sentir un peu comme Robinson Crusoë. Une expérience qu'on voudrait renouveler, qui émeut en tout cas et inspire durablement.

En las casi 750 hectáreas de la isla, a 32 kilómetros al noroeste de Mahé, se ha conseguido una simbiosis única entre la ecología y el lujo inteligente. Era necesario dar marcha atrás al reloj ecológico para recultivar esta isla que durante años estuvo inhabitada y abandonada. Once villas de 450 m² con todo el confort imaginable, ofrecen espacio suficiente para un máximo de 22 huéspedes, que tienen la oportunidad de contemplar el proyecto y de sentirse un poco como un robinson. Una experiencia que puede crear adicción pero que, después, conmueve e inspira.

Unica nel suo genere è la simbiosi fra ecologia e lusso intelligente realizzata sui quasi 750 ettari grande isola a 32 chilometri nordoccidentale a nord-ovest di Mahé. L'orologio ecologico deve essere tornato di nuovo indietro, l'isola rimasta per anni disabitata e inselvatichita deve essere ricoltivata coltivata di nuovo. Undici ville, da 450 m², provviste di ogni comodità possibile e immaginabile, offrono posto per 22 ospiti al massimo, che devono osservare il progetto ambizioso e potersi sentirsi allo tempo un po' come Robinson. Un'esperienza che può rendere dipendenti o per lo meno rimanere impressionare in modo duraturo e che può ispirare.

The architectural duo Silvio Rech and Lesley Carstens created a unique style for the resort, reflecting the essence of the natural environment.

Das Architektenpaar Silvio Rech und Lesley Carstens kreierte für das Resort einen eigenwilligen Stil, der das Wesen der natürlichen Umgebung widerspiegelt.

Le couple d'architectes Silvio Rech et Lesley Carstens ont créé pour ce resort un style volontaire parfaitement intégré à l'environnement naturel.

La pareja de arquitectos Silvio Rech y Lesley Carstens crearon para este complejo un estilo original que refleja el entorno natural de la construcción.

Gli architetti Silvio Rech und Lesley Carstens crearono per il resort uno stile estroso, che rispecchia lo spirito dell'ambiente naturale circostante.

Each of the eleven guest villas has a private pool, a 200 m² wooden terrace with an external bath and maximum privacy.

Jede der elf Gästevillen verfügt über einen Privatpool, eine 200 m² große Holzterrasse mit Außenbad und bietet ein Höchstmaß an Abgeschiedenheit.

Chacune des onze villas dispose d'une piscine privée, d'une terrasse de bois d'une superficie de 200 m² avec un bassin en plein air, pour une intimité absolument préservée.

Cada una de las once villas dispone de una piscina privada, de una terraza de madera de 200 m² con piscina exterior y ofrece una completa privacidad.

Ognuna delle undici ville dispone di una piscina privata, una veranda in legno di 200 m² attrezzata con bagno esterno, offrendo la massima discrezione per potersi appartare.

In the spa, *tailor-made treatments are offered to suit individual needs. They are meant to restore the balance of body, mind and soul.*

Im Spa *werden auf die individuellen Bedürfnisse zugeschnittene Behandlungen angeboten, die die Balance von Körper, Geist und Seele wiederherstellen sollen.*

Au Spa *sont dispensés des soins adaptés aux besoins individuels de chacun qui permettent de retrouver l'équilibre du corps, de l'esprit et de l'âme.*

En el spa *se ofrecen tratamientos completamente individualizados y adaptados a las necesidades de cada huésped, para recuperar el equilibrio entre el cuerpo, el espíritu y el alma.*

Nella SPA *vengono fatti trattamenti orientati alle esigenze individuali per ristabilire l'equilibrio fra corpo, spirito e anima.*

Taj Exotica Resort & Spa, Mauritius

Wolmar, Flic en Flac, Mauritius

As the only resort on Mauritius, the Taj Exotica, located on the west of the island on Wolmar Beach, consists entirely of villas. An eleven-hectare tropical park surrounds the 65 spacious villas and with their own pool they offer the perfect setting for relaxation. From the terrace, guests enjoy a view far out to sea and of the colorful coral reef that surrounds the island. In the 2,000 m² Jiva Spa, Ayurvedic and western practices are combined.

Als einziges Resort auf Mauritius besteht das im Westen der Insel am Wolmar Beach gelegene Taj Exotica ausschließlich aus Villen. Umgeben von einem elf Hektar großen tropischen Park bieten die 65 großzügig geschnittenen Villen mit eigenem Pool den perfekten Rahmen zum Entspannen. Von der Terrasse aus genießt man einen weiten Blick auf das Meer und das farbenprächtige Korallenriff, das die Insel umgibt. Im 2.000 m² großen Jiva Spa werden ayurvedische und westliche Anwendungen kombiniert.

Ce resort situé sur la côte ouest de l'île le long de la plage Wolmar est le seul de Maurice à être exclusivement composé de villas. Entourées d'un parc tropical de onze hectares, les 65 villas très spacieuses dotées d'une piscine privée constituent un cadre parfait pour la détente. De la terrasse on jouit d'une large vue sur la mer et le récif corallien aux magnifiques couleurs entourant l'île. Le Jiva Spa d'une superficie de 2 000 m² associe traitements ayurvédiques et soins occidentaux.

El Taj Exotica es el único complejo hotelero de la isla Mauricio y está situado en su parte occidental. El hotel se compone de 65 grandes villas rodeadas de un parque tropical de once hectáreas. Cada una de las casas posee una piscina privada y ofrece el escenario ideal para descansar. Desde la terraza se disfruta de una extensa vista sobre el mar y el colorido arrecife de coral que rodea la isla. En el balneario Jiva, de 2000 m², se combinan tratamientos de ayurveda con otros occidentales.

Quale unica struttura su Mauritius, il resort Taj Exotica, ubicato a ovest dell'isola a Wolmar Beach, si compone esclusivamente di ville. Le 65 ville, circondate da un parco tropicale di undici ettari, molto spaziose, con piscina privata, offrono l'ambiente ideale per rilassarsi. Dalla terrazza si gode un'ampia vista sul mare e sullo sfarzo dei colori della barriera corallina che circonda l'isola. Nella Jiva-SPA, che si estende per 2000 m², si alternano e si mescolano i vari trattamenti ayurvedici con quelli occidentali.

Contemporary design, beyond a superimposed folklore image, dominates the interior of the Breaker's Bar.

Zeitgemäßes Design jenseits aufgesetzter Folklore dominiert das Interieur der Breaker's Bar.

Un design contemporain loin de tout folklore caricatural caractérise l'intérieur du Breaker's Bar.

Un diseño moderno alejado de las imitaciones folclorísticas domina la decoración del interior del Breaker's Bar.

Un moderno design, al di là di ogni obbligato folclore, domina l'interno dil Breaker's Bar.

Daybeds and idyllic shady spots invite to relax at the poolside.

Tagesbetten und schattenspendende Plätze laden zum Relaxen am Pool ein.

Des larges chaises longues et des places ombrageuses invitent à la détente au bord de la piscine.

Cómodas tumbonas y lugares umbríos invitan al relajamiento en la zona de la piscina.

Commodi lettini e posti ombrosi invitano al rilassamento puro alla piscina.

Le Prince Maurice

Poste de Flacq, Mauritius

The property lies on a peninsula on the northeast coast of Mauritius, in the midst of luscious exotic vegetation. It attempts to evoke times past when seafarers still landed here to trade spices: modern elements such as a computer at the reception desk were skillfully concealed behind sheets of glass and documents kept in two wooden chests. Different suites can be chosen—the largest measures 350 m² and offers a private patio, an open-air bath and two pools.

Auf einer Halbinsel an der Nordostküste von Mauritius liegt das Anwesen inmitten üppiger exotischer Vegetation. Es versucht vergangene Zeiten heraufzubeschwören, als noch Seefahrer wegen des Gewürzhandels hier anlegten: Moderne Elemente wie der Computer an der Rezeption werden geschickt hinter dunklen Glasplatten verborgen und Dokumente in zwei Holztruhen aufbewahrt. Unterschiedliche Suiten stehen zur Auswahl, die größte misst 350 m² und bietet einen privaten Patio, ein Open-Air-Bad und zwei Pools.

Le domaine se trouve sur une presqu'île, sur la côte nord-est de l'île Maurice, niché au milieu d'une végétation exotique dense. Il évoque l'époque révolue où les marins débarquaient ici pour le commerce des épices : les éléments modernes comme l'ordinateur de la réception sont adroitement dissimulés derrière des plaques de verre sombres et des documents conservées dans deux coffres en bois. Différentes suites peuvent être choisies ; la plus grande, d'une superficie de 350 m², est dotée d'un patio privé, d'une salle de bains en plein air et de deux piscines.

En una península, en la costa noreste de Mauricio, está ubicado este hotel, en medio de una exuberante vegetación exótica. El establecimiento intenta evocar épocas pasadas, cuando los marineros anclaban aquí, debido al comercio de especias. Elementos de la modernidad, como el ordenador en la recepción, se esconden hábilmente tras placas de vidrio oscuro y documentos se mantienen en un cofre de madera. Hay diferentes suites para elegir y la más grande de éstas es de 350 m² y cuenta con un patio interior privado, bañera a cielo raso y dos piscinas.

La tenuta si trova su una peninsola sulla costa Nord-Est di Mauritius, in mezzo ad una rigogliosa vegetazione esotica. Si tenta d'evocare i tempi passati quando i marinai vi approdavano per il commercio delle spezie. Elementi moderni come i computer della reception sono stati nascosti dietro a piastre di vetro scuro e documenti sono depositate in due cassoni di legno. Sono a disposizione diverse suites, la più grande misura 350 m² ed offre un patio privato, un bagno all'aperto e due piscine.

In design terms, the resort belongs to the most beautiful on the island. It is named after the German aristocrat, Prince Mauritz of Oranien and Nassau.

Gestalterisch gehört das Resort zu den schönsten der Insel. Benannt ist es nach dem deutschen Aristokraten Prinz Mauritz von Oranien und Nassau.

Par sa conception le Resort est l'un des plus beaux de l'île. Il tient son nom d'un aristocrate allemand, le Prince Mauritz von Oranien und Nassau.

Por su diseño éste es uno de los complejos hoteleros más bellos de la isla. Le debe su nombre al príncipe alemán Mauritz von Oranien und Nassau.

La forma del resort è una delle più belle dell'isola. Ha preso il nome dall'aristocratico tedesco "Prinz Mauritz von Oranien und Nassau".

In spite of the traditional building style and partly antique furniture, the hotel complex with its 89 suites appears very modern in architectural terms.

Trotz der traditionellen Bauweise und teilweise antiker Möbel wirkt die Hotelanlage mit ihren 89 Suiten architektonisch sehr modern.

Malgré la construction traditionnelle et certains meubles antiques, la propriété, avec ses 89 suites, laisse une impression architecturale très moderne.

A pesar del estilo tradicional de su construcción y de la antigüedad de alguno de sus muebles, esta instalación hotelera con 89 suites parece muy moderna desde el punto de vista arquitectónico.

Nonostante la costruzione tradizionale e, in parte, i mobili antichi, l'impianto residenziale dà con le sue 89 suites un'impressione di moderno.

At dusk the excellent lighting design turns the resort in a mood of a romantic fairy tale.

Beispielhaftes Lichtdesign verwandelt die Anlage mit der Dämmerung in eine romantische Märchenwelt.

Au crépuscule l'excellente conception d'éclairage tourne le resort dans une humeur d'un conte de fées romantique.

Al ocaso el excelente diseño de iluminación da un modo romántico de cuento de hadas a este lugar vacacional.

All'imbrunire il disegno eccellente di illuminazione gira il resort in un umore di un racconto fairy romantico.

The Oberoi Mauritius

Turtle Bay, Mauritius

The unique cultural mix of African, Asian and European influence on Mauritius is reflected in the architecture and design of this hotel complex, with its 73 villas and terrace-pavilions. The roofs are thatched with dried sugar cane, the walls are constructed of volcanic rock, and African objets d'art set the tone in the rooms. This refuge lies in total seclusion on the island's northwest coast, directly on Turtle Bay, although the busy island capital of Port Louis is only 20 minutes away by car.

Der einzigartige kulturelle Mix aus afrikanischen, asiatischen und europäischen Einflüssen auf Mauritius spiegelt sich in der Architektur und dem Design der Hotelanlage mit ihren 73 Villen und Terrassen-Pavillons wider. Die Dächer wurden mit getrocknetem Zuckerrohr gedeckt, die Mauern sind aus Vulkangestein gefertigt, afrikanische Kunstgegenstände setzen in den Zimmern Akzente. Das Refugium liegt in völliger Abgeschiedenheit an der Nordwestküste der Insel, direkt am Baie aux Tortues, trotzdem erreicht man die quirlige Inselhauptstadt Port Louis in nur 20 Autominuten.

Le mélange culturel unique des influences africaines, asiatiques et européennes sur l'île Maurice se reflète dans l'architecture et la conception de cet ensemble de 73 villas et petits pavillons. Les toits sont recouverts de canne à sucre séchée, les murs sont édifiés en pierre volcanique et des objets d'art africains créent le contraste dans les chambres. Ce havre de paix est complètement isolé sur la côte nord-ouest de l'île, directement au bord de la baie aux tortues ; on rejoint pourtant Port Louis, la remuante capitale de l'île, en seulement 20 minutes en voiture.

La excepcional mezcla cultural de influencias africanas, asiáticas y europeas presente en Mauricio, se refleja en la arquitectura y el diseño de este complejo hotelero con sus 73 villas y sus pabellones. Los tejados están recubiertos con cañas de azúcar secas, los muros han sido elaborados con piedras volcánicas y los objetos de arte africanos ponen el acento artístico en las habitaciones. Este refugio se encuentra en un lugar completamente apartado, en la costa noroeste de la isla, en la Baie aux Tortues. Aún así es posible llegar a la animada capital de la isla, Port Louis, en sólo 20 minutos en coche.

La singolare mescolanza di cultura africana, asiatica ed europea si rispecchia nell'architettura e nel design dell'impianto residenziale con le sue 73 ville e terrazze-padiglioni. I tetti furono coperti con canna da zucchero essiccata, per la costruzione delle mura è stata usata pietra lavica, oggetti d'arte africana danno alle camere un tocco particolare. Il rifugio giace completamente isolato sulla costa nord-ovest dell'isola, direttamente sulla Baie aux Tortues, ciò nonostante si arriva in soli 20 minuti d'auto alla vivacissima capitale dell'isola Port Louis.

Natural materials and finely graded, light color shades give the suites, which measure up to 650 m², a light atmosphere.

Natürliche Materialien und fein abgestufte helle Farbschattierungen verleihen den bis zu 650 m² großen Suiten eine lichte Atmosphäre.

Des matériaux naturels et des dégradés de teintes claires confèrent aux vastes suites allant jusqu'à 650 m² de superficie une atmosphère lumineuse.

Materiales naturales y colores claros finamente matizados dotan a las suites de hasta 650 m² de un ambiente luminoso.

Materiale naturale e delicate sfumature nella gradazione dei colori donano alle suites, grandi 650 m², un'atmosfera chiara e luminosa.

Here water becomes an element of architectural design: the surface of the pool and ponds around the restaurant optically merge with the Indian Ocean.

Hier wird Wasser zum architektonischen Gestaltungselement: die Oberfläche des Pools und der Teiche um das Restaurant verschmelzen optisch mit dem Indischen Ozean.

Ici l'eau est un élément de la conception architecturale : la surface de la piscine et des bassins autour du restaurant se fondent visuellement dans l'océan indien.

Aquí el agua se convierte en un elemento arquitectónico: la superficie de la piscina y de los estanques que rodean al restaurante parece fundirse con el Océano Índico.

Qui l'acqua diventa un elemento di creazione architettonica: la superficie della piscina e gli stagni attorno al ristorante sembrano fondersi con l'Oceano Indiano.

112   The Oberoi Mauritius *Turtle Bay, Mauritius*

The suites are marked by a restrained, contemporary elegance. Sixteen of them have their own private pools.

Die Suiten sind geprägt von einer zurückhaltenden zeitgemäßen Eleganz, 16 davon besitzen einen eigenen Swimmingpool.

Les suites sont imprégnées d'une élégance contemporaine discrète, seize d'entre elles disposent d'une piscine individuelle.

Las suites están impregnadas de una moderna y discreta elegancia, 16 de ellas disponen de una piscina privada.

Le suites delle quali 16 hanno una piscina a sé, sono di un'eleganza discreta e moderna.

Ngorongoro Crater Lodge
Ngorongoro Conservation Area, Tanzania

Known as Africa's Versailles: Here in this noble lodge traditional building styles and eccentric safari-baroque clash with each other. Clay huts with palm roofs cling to the over 2,000 meter-high crater edge of the Ngorongoro with its unique fauna. Crystal chandeliers hang from the banana-leaf roofs in the suites, silk curtains shimmer in front of panoramic windows, brocade cushions decorate four-poster beds from Zanzibar. But that's not all: a butler brings tea to your bedside, lights the fire and scatters rose petals into the bath water.

Bekannt ist die noble Lodge als das afrikanische Versailles: Hier prallen traditionelle Bauweise und exzentrischer Safari-Barock aufeinander. Palmen gedeckte Lehmhütten schmiegen sich an den über 2.000 Meter hohen Kraterrand des Ngorongoro mit seiner einzigartigen Fauna. In den Suiten hängen Kristalllüster von Bananenblattdächern, vor den Panoramafenstern glänzen Seidengardinen, Brokatkissen zieren Himmelbetten aus Sansibar. Doch damit nicht genug: Ein Butler bringt Tee ans Bett, zündet den Kamin an und streut Rosenblätter ins Badewasser.

Ce lodge passe pour être la Versailles africaine: construction traditionnelle et style safari baroque s'y rencontrent. Des cases d'argile recouvertes de feuilles de palmier se serrent sur les flancs du cratère du Ngorongoro à plus de 2 000 m d'altitude avec sa faune exceptionnelle. Dans les suites, des lustres en cristal sont suspendus aux toits de feuilles de bananier, des rideaux de soie scintillent devant les fenêtres panoramiques, des coussins de brocart ornent les baldaquins de Zanzibar. Mais ce n'est pas tout : le majordome apporte le thé au pied du lit, allume la cheminée et répand des pétales de rose dans l'eau du bain.

A este elegante lodge se le conoce como el Versalles africano: aquí los estilos arquitectónicos tradicionales chocan con el excéntrico "barroco de safari". Cabañas de adobe cubiertas con palmas se apiñan en el borde del cráter del Ngorongoro, a más de 2000 metros de altura, rodeadas de una extraordinaria fauna. En las suites cuelgan arañas de cristal de los techos de hojas de palma, delante de las ventanas panorámicas cuelgan brillantes cortinas de seda, cojines brocados adornan las camas con dosel de Zanzíbar. Pero eso no es todo: un mayordomo lleva el té a la cama, enciende la chimenea y esparce hojas de rosa en la bañera.

La lodge, signorile e distinta, è conosciuta come la Versailles africana. Qui si scontrano la costruzione tradizionale con l'eccentrico safari barocco. Capanne d'argilla coperte da palme s'addossano all'orlo del cratere del Ngorongoro, alto più di 2000 metri con la sua fauna incomparabile. Nelle suites pendono lampadari di cristallo da tetti fatti con foglie di banano, davanti alle finestre panoramiche luccicano tende di seta, cuscini di broccato ornano i letti a baldacchino di Zanzibar. Ma non è tutto: un maggiordomo serve il tè a letto, accende il camino e cosparge l'acqua nella vasca da bagno di petali di rose.

Silvio Rech and Lesley Carstens have let inspiration grow from the breathtaking nature. With natural forms and wild material combinations, the architectural duo created a unique living environment with all the luxury you can imagine.

Silvio Rech und Lesley Carstens haben sich von der atemberaubenden Natur inspirieren lassen. Mit urwüchsigen Formen und wilden Material-kombinationen schuf das Architektenpaar eine einzigartige Wohnumgebung mit allem erdenklichen Luxus.

Silvio Rech et Lesley Carstens se sont laissés inspirer par une nature sublime. A l'aide de formes primitives et de combinaisons de matériaux sauvages le couple d'architecte a créé un environnement recherché où ne manque aucun élément de luxe.

Silvio Rech y Lesley Carstens se han dejado inspirar por una naturaleza espectacular. A partir de formas naturales y extraordinarias combinaciones de materiales, esta pareja de arquitectos creó un entorno único en las viviendas con todo el lujo imaginable.

Silvio Rech e Lesley Carstens si sono lasciati ispirare dalla natura che mozza il respiro. Con forme robuste e primitive e selvagge combinazioni di materiale gli architetti hanno creato un ambiente residenziale unico con ogni lusso possibile ed immaginabile.

Downstairs a Parisian plush apartment, upstairs an African hut with a wooden slate roof. These contrasts may appear decadent, but anyone who personally experiences the rooms will find them amazingly harmonious and fitting for the environment.

Unten Pariser *Plüschwohnung, oben afrikanische Hütte mit Holzschindeldecke. Diese Gegensätze mögen dekadent wirken, aber wer die Räume persönlich erlebt, findet sie verblüffend harmonisch und zur Umgebung passend.*

En bas appartement *parisien avec peluche, en haut case africaine avec plafond à bardeaux de bois. Ces contrastes peuvent paraître décadents, mais quiconque investit ces lieux est stupéfait par leur harmonie et leur intégration à l'environnement.*

Abajo, una *vivienda parisina con elementos afelpados, arriba, una cabaña africana con techo de ripias de madera. Estos contrastes pueden parecer decadentes, pero después de alojarse aquí el visitante los encuentra increíblemente armoniosos y adaptados al entorno.*

Sotto c'è *l'abitazione parigina - peluche, sopra c'è la capanna africana con soffitto in scandole di legno. Questi contrasti possono anche sembrare decadenti, ma chi ne fa l'esperienza personale, trova che le camere sono di un'armonia sbalorditiva e senz'altro adattate all'ambiente.*

Ngorongoro Crater Lodge Ngorongoro Conservation Area, Tanzania   118

Lake Manyara Tree Lodge

Lake Manyara National Park, Tanzania

The comfortable huts in the lodge are hidden under the old mahogany trees near Manyara lake—a wildlife park, which is famous for its tree lions. Chris Browne designed the interior: originally carved bush spirits lean against modern kitchen bars on the lunch deck, where chefs let you peek in their pots. Minimalist Zebrano wood chairs are placed in front of antique doors from Zanzibar. In the evenings, the lights from the paraffin lamps illuminate the dining table like hundreds of dancing glowworms.

Die komfortablen Hütten der Lodge verstecken sich unter den alten Mahagonibäumen nahe des Manyara-Sees – ein Wildpark, der berühmt ist für seine Baumlöwen. Das Interieur konzipierte der Südafrikaner Chris Browne: Urige geschnitzte Buschgeister lehnen am modernen Küchentresen auf dem Lunch-Deck, wo sich die Köche in die Töpfe gucken lassen. Minimalistische Stühle aus Zebranoholz stehen vor antiken Türen aus Sansibar. Abends beleuchten die Lichter der Petroleumlampen die Dinnertafel wie hunderte tanzender Glühwürmchen.

Les confortables chalets du lodge sont nichés sous les vieux acajous de la forêt proche du lac Manyara – un parc national célèbre pour ses lions qui dorment dans les arbres. L'intérieur a été conçu par le Sud-africain Chris Browne : d'étranges sculptures d'esprits de la brousse sont accoudées au comptoir d'une cuisine moderne sur la terrasse du déjeuner où l'on peut observer les cuisiniers. Des chaises minimalistes en bois zébrano sont disposées devant d'antiques portes de Zanzibar. Le soir, les flammes dansantes des lampes à pétrole éclairent les tables du dîner comme des centaines de vers luisants.

Las cómodas cabañas del lodge se esconden bajo las viejas caobas, cerca del lago Manyara, un parque natural famoso por sus leones trepadores. El sudafricano Chris Browne diseñó su interior: espíritus del bosque tallados en madera se apoyan en la moderna barra de la cocina, en la terraza del comedor, donde los cocineros permiten que se les observe mientras cocinan. Sillas minimalistas de madera zebrano están colocadas delante de antiguas puertas de Zanzíbar. Por la tarde, las lámparas de petróleo alumbran el comedor como si fueran miles de luciérnagas.

Le confortevoli capanne del lodge sono nascoste sotto vecchi alberi di mogano nelle vicinanze del lago Manyara – una riserva di caccia, famosa per i leoni che si arrampicano sugli alberi. L'interno è stato concepito dal sudafricano Chris Browne: originali strani spiriti della foresta s'appoggiano al banco della moderna cucina lì dove si serve il lunch e dove i cuochi si fanno guardare nelle pentole. Sedie minimalistiche di legno zebra sono messe davanti ad antiche porte di Zanzibar. La sera le luci delle lampade a petrolio illuminano, come centinaia di lucciole danzanti, le tavole apparecchiate per il dinner.

For lunch, guests meet on the terrace in front of the open kitchen. At dinner, a fence made of branches protects from wild animals.

Zum Lunch *trifft man sich auf der Terrasse vor der offenen Küche. Beim Dinner bietet ein Zaun aus Ästen Schutz vor Wildtieren.*

Au déjeuner *on se rencontre sur la terrasse devant la cuisine ouverte. Au dîner une clôture de branchage protège les convives des bêtes sauvages.*

El almuerzo *tiene lugar en la terraza, delante de la cocina abierta. Durante la cena, una cerca de ramas protege a los comensales de los animales salvajes.*

Per il *lunch ci si incontra sulla terrazza davanti alla cucina all'aperto. Per il dinner un recinto fatto di rami d'albero protegge dagli animali selvatici.*

Four-poster beds invite you to relax in the airy tree houses. Unforgettable: a bath in the tub underneath the mahogany treetops.

Himmelbetten laden in den luftigen Baumhäusern zum Entspannen ein. Unvergesslich: Ein Bad in der Wanne unter den Wipfeln der Mahagonibäume.

Des lits à baldaquin invitent au repos dans les chalets aérés construits dans les arbres. Inoubliable: le bain dans la baignoire sous la cime des acajous.

En las casas de madera, las camas con dosel invitan a relajarse. Inolvidable: Un baño en la bañera bajo las copas de las caobas.

Letti a baldacchino nelle case – albero ariose invitano a rilassarsi. Indimenticabile: un bagno nella vasca sotto le cime dei mogani.

Lake Manyara Tree Lodge *Lake Manyara National Park, Tanzania* 123

Designer furniture *beneath a banana leaf roof, old wooden boats at the entrance gate—the lodge's individual style combination is unique.*

Designermöbel *unter einem Bananenblattdach, alte Holzboote am Eingangstor – der individuelle Stilmix der Lodge ist einzigartig.*

Des meubles *de designer sous un toit de feuilles de bananier, de vieux bateaux de bois à l'entrée – l'original mariage des styles du lodge est unique.*

Muebles de *diseño bajo los techos de hojas de palmera, viejas barcas de madera en la puerta de la entrada; esta particular mezcla de estilos del lodge es única.*

Mobili di *design sotto il tetto di foglie di banano, vecchie barche di legno davanti alla porta d'entrata – l'individuale mescolanza di stili nei lodge è incomparabile.*

Wolwedans

NamibRand, Namibia

Endless space and peace—as you don't find anywhere else in the world—is on offer from the three camps of the Wolwedans Collection, located in the heart of the Namib-Rand Nature Reserve 400 km south west of Windhoek. No whirr of the air conditioning, no electrical gadget disturbs the unpretentious, direct experience of the desert. Here, up-front luxury has been deliberately avoided. You can live in tents, erected on wooden platforms, or in the comfortable wooden chalets.

Grenzenlose Weite und Stille, wie man sie vielleicht nirgendwo sonst auf der Welt findet, bieten die drei im Herzen des NamibRand Naturreservats gelegenen Camps der Wolwedans-Collection 400 km südwestlich von Windhoek. Keine surrende Klimaanlage, kein elektrisches Gerät stören das unverfälschte unmittelbare Wüstenerlebnis. Auf vordergründigen Luxus wurde hier bewusst verzichtet. Wohnen kann man in auf hölzernen Plattformen errichteten Zelten oder in den aus Holz konstruierten komfortablen Chalets.

Étendues à perte de vue et sérénité telles qu'elles n'existent peut-être nulle part ailleurs au mode vous attendent dans les trois camps, au cœur du parc naturel Namib-Rand, de la collection Wolwedans, à 400 km au sud-ouest de Windhoek. Aucun bourdonnement de climatisation, aucun appareil électrique ne perturbe cette authentique expérience immédiate du désert. Ici on a sciemment renoncé à tout luxe superficiel. L'hébergement se fait dans des tentes montées sur pilotis ou de confortables chalets en bois.

Extensión y tranquilidad ilimitadas, seguramente únicas en el mundo, esto es lo que ofrecen los tres campamentos de la Wolwedans Collection, en el corazón de la reserva natural del NamibRand, 400 km al sudoeste de Windhoek. Una auténtica experiencia en el desierto sin el zumbido del aire acondicionado y sin equipos eléctricos. Aquí se ha renunciado de forma consciente al lujo superficial. Los huéspedes pueden alojarse en tiendas levantadas sobre plataformas de madera o en cómodos chalés también de madera.

Spazi sconfinati e silenzio, come forse non sono da trovare in nessun altro posto al mondo, offrono i tre campi della Wolwedans-Collection 400 km a sudovest di Windhoek nel cuore della riserva naturale NamibRand. Nessun impianto ronzante di aria condizionata, nessun elettrodomestico disturba questa esperienza, immediata e pura, che si fa nel deserto. Si è rinunciato consapevolmente al lusso in prima linea. Abitare si può in tende piantate su piattaforme in legno o nei comodi chalet.

Minimalist fascination—the exterior and interior rooms merge smoothly into each other. The terrace is the essential part of the chalets, constructed in an easy wooden building style,—so to speak, your living room right in the middle of nature.

Karge Faszination —Außen- und Innenräume gehen nahtlos ineinander über. Wesentlicher Bestandteil der in leichter Holzbauweise erstellten Chalets ist die Terrasse, sozusagen das Wohnzimmer inmitten der Natur.

Aride fascination – où s'imbriquent espaces intérieur et extérieur. La terrasse représente le principal élément des chalets en bois de construction légère, un living en pleine nature.

Sencillez fascinante – los espacios exteriores e interiores se entrelazan sin fisuras. El elemento más importante de los chalés, fabricados con una estructura ligera de madera, es la terraza, un cuarto de estar en medio de la naturaleza.

Fascino senza fronzoli – gli spazi all'esterno sono tutt'uno con quelli interni. La parte essenziale dei chalet di leggera costruzione in legno è la terrazza, che sarebbe, per così dire, un camera di soggiorno nel bel mezzo della natura.

Wolwedans incorporates the Dunes Lodge with nine chalets, the MountainView suite measuring 200 m², the Private Camp as well as the luxurious tent accommodation of Dune Camp.

Wolwedans umfasst die Dunes Lodge mit neun Chalets, die 200 m² große MountainView Suite, das Private Camp sowie die luxuriösen Zeltunterkünfte des Dune Camps.

Wolwedans comprend le Dunes Lodge avec neuf chalets, la suite MountainView de 200 m², le Private Camp ainsi que le luxueux hébergement en tentes du Dune Camp.

Wolwedans está formado por el Dunes Lodge con nueve chalés, la suite MountainView, de 200 m², el Private Camp y las lujosas tiendas del Dune Camp.

Wolwedans comprende i Dune Lodge con nove chalet, la suite MountainView di 200 m², il campo privato e i lussuosi alloggi tendati dei Dune Camps.

Sossusvlei Mountain Lodge

NamibRand, Namibia

The red dunes of Sossusvlei with their sharp-edged ridges are considered Africa's most beautiful desert dunes. They gave the unusual lodge its name. The lodge is located in the middle of the 184,000-hectare NamibRand Nature Reserve. The luxurious guest villas built out of natural stone and belonging to the lodge, which is built on a mountain slope, offer an undistorted view across the vast, imposing desert landscape due to their ceiling-high front windows. The stargazing safaris that are run by American astronomical experts are unique.

Die roten Dünen des Sossusvlei, die mit ihren scharfkantigen Graten als die schönsten Wüstendünen Afrikas gelten, gaben der ungewöhnlichen Lodge inmitten des 184 000 Hektar großen NamibRand Naturreservats den Namen. Die aus Naturstein gebauten luxuriösen Gästevillen der an einen Berghang gebauten Lodge bieten mit ihren raumhohen Frontscheiben ungehinderte Sicht über die weite imposante Wüstenlandschaft. Einzigartig sind die von amerikanischen Astronomie-Spezialisten begleiteten Sternbeobachtungs-Safaris.

Les dunes rouges du Sossusvlei réputées pour leurs arêtes vives et passant pour les plus belles d'Afrique ont donné leur nom à ce lodge insolite situé au cœur du parc naturel NamibRand qui s'étend sur 184 000 hectares. Les luxueuses villas de pierre de ce lodge construit à flanc de montagne, avec leurs vitres aussi hautes que les pièces, permettent de profiter de ce paysage désertique imposant. Les safaris d'observation des étoiles accompagnés par des spécialistes astronomes américains sont exceptionnels.

Las dunas rojas del Sossusvlei, consideradas como las dunas más bellas de África por sus crestas afiladas, dan nombre a este extraordinario complejo situado en medio de la reserva natural NamibRand, de 184.000 hectáreas de extensión. Las lujosas villas de piedra natural del lodge, levantado en la falda de la montaña, ofrecen una vista libre del impresionante paisaje del desierto gracias a sus fachadas de cristal. Los safaris para observar las estrellas son algo único y se realizan en compañía de astrónomos estadounidenses.

Le dune rosse di Sossusvlei, barcane con creste tanto nitide da sembrare affilate, sono considerate le più belle delle dune africane e hanno dato il nome allo straordinario lodge al centro della riserva naturale NamibRand, estesa per 184 000 ettari. Le lussuose ville, costruite in pietra naturale e facenti parte di un lodge ai pendii di una montagna, offrono agli ospiti, attraverso i vetri alti quanto la parete, una vista incontrastata sul paesaggio vasto e imponente. Unici nel loro genere sono i safari organizzati per osservare le stelle. Le escursioni sono accompagnate da americani esperti in astronomia.

All around the main lodge, which houses the restaurant as well as a bar and lounge-lobby, 10 desert villas are arranged. When the temperatures sink at night, the fire blazes in the hearth.

Rund um die Hauptlodge, die das Restaurant sowie eine Bar und Lobbylounge beherbergen, gruppieren sich 10 Wüstenvillen. Wenn nachts die Temperaturen sinken, lodert das Feuer im Kamin.

Autour du lodge principal qui abrite le restaurant, le bar et le salon de la réception se groupent les 10 villas. Quand les températures baissent la nuit, un feu flamboie dans la cheminée.

Alrededor del complejo principal, donde se alojan el restaurante, el bar y el salón del vestíbulo, se agrupan 10 villas. Cuando por la noche descienden las temperaturas, el fuego arde en la chimenea.

Intorno al lodge principale, dove si trova il ristorante come pure un bar e una Lobby Lounge, sono raggruppate 10 ville adattate al deserto. Quando la notte si abbassa la temperatura, arde il fuoco nel camino.

From the lodge's terrace, guests look out at the endless expanse of the spectacular sand dunes.

Von der Terrasse der Lodge aus blickt man auf die endlose Weite der spektakulären Sanddünen.

De la terrasse du lodge le regard se perd sur les éblouissantes dunes de sable.

Desde la terraza del lodge se disfruta de la inmensidad de las espectaculares dunas.

Dalla terrazza del lodge si guarda sulla distesa sterminata delle dune di sabbia.

Sossusvlei Mountain Lodge *NamibRand, Namibia*   133

Mowani Mountain Camp

Twyfelfontein, Namibia

On a rocky elevation with a wide view across an archaic landscape, the camp is perfectly nestled between the giant erratic-shaped rocks in Twyfelfontein Nature Reserve in Namibia's north. The camp is built in the style of an African village. The twelve luxurious tents as well as two luxury huts with dome-shaped roofs covered in thatch, which take on the shape of the surrounding granite formations, were built on wooden platforms. They are the perfect base from which to discover well up to 2,000 cliff engravings and murals, which the people who settled in this region 6,000 years ago left behind them.

Auf einer felsigen Anhöhe mit weitem Blick über eine archaische Landschaft, vollkommen eingebettet zwischen den riesigen Findlingen im Twyfelfontein Naturschutzgebiet im Norden Namibias liegt das im Stil eines afrikanischen Dorfes gebaute Camp. Die zwölf luxuriösen Zeltunterkünfte sowie zwei Luxushütten mit kuppelartigen Reet gedeckten Dächern, die die Form der umgebenden Granitgesteinsformationen aufnehmen, wurden auf hölzernen Plattformen errichtet. Sie sind die perfekte Basis, die gut 2.000 Felsengravuren und Malereien zu entdecken, welche die Menschen hinterließen, die diese Region vor 6.000 Jahren besiedelten.

Sur une hauteur rocheuse procurant une large vue sur un paysage archaïque, enchâssé parmi les blocs erratiques du parc naturel Twyfelfontein au nord de la Namibie se trouve le camp construit à la manière d'un village africain. Les douze luxueuses tentes et les deux somptueuses cases au toit de chaume arrondi qui adoptent le dessin des formations granitiques environnantes ont été construites sur pilotis. C'est le point de départ idéal pour découvrir les quelque 2 000 gravures et peintures rupestres laissées par les peuplades de ces régions il y a 6 000 ans.

Este campamento, cuya construcción evoca el estilo de un pueblo africano, está situado entre bloques erráticos, en la reserva natural Twyfelfontein, al norte de Namibia, sobre una elevación rocosa desde donde se disfruta de una amplia vista sobre el primitivo paisaje. Las doce lujosas tiendas y las dos suntuosas cabañas con tejados de caña con forma de cúpula, han sido construidas sobre plataformas de madera y mimetizan la forma de las formaciones graníticas circundantes. En estas rocas se pueden descubrir los casi 2000 grabados y pinturas que dejaron los pobladores de esta región hace 6000 años.

Su una rocciosa altura con ampia e larga vista sul paesaggio arcaico, perfettamente integrato fra i giganteschi massi erratici nel parco nazionale Twyfelfontein nel nord della Namibia, è ubicato il Camp, costruito nello stile di un villaggio africano. I dodici alloggi lussuosi come pure due capanne di lusso coperte da tetti di paglia a cupola – che assumono la forma delle formazioni di roccia granitica circostanti – sono stati eretti su palafitte di legno e sono il punto di partenza per andare alla scoperta delle ben 2000 incisioni nella roccia e delle pitture di arte rupestre, che la popolazione, vissuta in questa regione 6000 anni fa, ci ha lasciato.

Between the bizarre cliff formations, the little thatch-roofed houses look like a part of nature.

Zwischen den bizarren Felsformationen wirken die reetgedeckten Häuschen wie ein Teil der Natur.

Entre les étranges formations rocheuses les cases aux toits de paille sont partie intégrante de la nature.

Entre las extrañas formaciones rocosas, las casitas cubiertas de paja parecen ser parte de la naturaleza.

Fra le bizzarre formazioni rocciose le casette ricoperti di paglia sembrano far parte della natura.

African art and rustic interior architecture are combined to a new aesthetic, completed by an open-air bath situated right in the middle of the prairie grass landscape.

Afrikanische Kunst und eine rustikale Innenarchitektur verbinden sich zu einer neuen Ästhetik, die ein Bad inmitten der Steppenlandschaft vervollständigt.

Art africain et architecture intérieure rustique aboutissent à une esthétique nouvelle que vient compléter un bain au cœur de ce paysage de steppes.

El arte africano y el rústico diseño interior se funden en una nueva estética que se completa con un baño en medio del paisaje estepario.

Arte africana e la rusticale parte architettonica interna formano insieme una nuova estetica che viene completata da un bagno nel bel mezzo del paesaggio della steppa.

136   Mowani Mountain Camp *Twyfelfontein, Namibia*

Cape Grace

Cape Town, South Africa

The hotel alone is already worth a visit,—this is how many prominent guests like Bill Clinton rave about the place and it's also true of the spectacular location: the elegant hotel is situated on the picturesque Victoria & Alfred Waterfront on a private quay with a view of the marina and Table Mountain. It is furnished with lots of attention to detail: fresh flowers, warm-colored fabrics and 2,000 artworks create an intimate ambiance—it's like you are a guest staying with good friends.

Schon das Hotel selbst ist eine Reise wert, schwärmen viele prominente Gäste wie Bill Clinton auch wegen der spektakulären Lage: Das elegante Hotel liegt an der malerischen Victoria & Alfred Waterfront an einem Privatkai mit Blick auf Yachthafen und Tafelberg. Eingerichtet ist es mit viel Liebe zum Detail: Frische Blumen, Stoffe in warmen Farben und 2.000 Kunstwerke kreieren ein familiäres Ambiente — so als wäre man bei guten Freunden zu Gast.

L'hôtel en soi vaut le voyage, affirment avec enthousiasme de nombreux hôtes célèbres tels que Bill Clinton – ne serait-ce que pour son emplacement spectaculaire : cet élégant hôtel est situé le long de la pittoresque Victoria & Alfred Waterfront sur un quai privé avec vue sur le port de plaisance et la Table Mountain. Le décor témoigne de l'amour du détail : fleurs fraîches, étoffes aux tons chaleureux et 2 000 œuvres d'art créent une atmosphère familiale – comme si l'on était invité par de vieux amis.

Muchos de sus famosos huéspedes, como Bill Clinton, afirman que sólo para ver el hotel merece la pena el viaje, pero también por su espectacular ubicación: El elegante hotel está situado en el pintoresco paseo Victoria & Alfred, en un muelle privado con vistas al puerto de yates y a la meseta. Su decoración demuestra una gran atención a los detalles: las flores frescas, las telas en colores calorosos y las más de 2000 obras de arte, crean un ambiente familiar, como si se estuviera alojado en la casa de unos buenos amigos.

Già solo l'albergo vale la pena di un viaggio, dicono entusiasti molti ospiti prominenti come Bill Clinton – anche a causa della sua posizione sensazionale: l'elegante albergo si trova al famoso lungo-mare Victoria & Alfred Waterfront con vista sul porto degli yacht e sulla "Table Mountain". È arredato con molto amore per il dettaglio: fiori freschi, stoffe in colori caldorosi e 2000 opere d'arte creano un ambiente familiare – come se si fosse ospiti di buoni amici.

Floor-to-ceiling windows in the elegant suites open up the view of the international yachting harbor.

Bodentiefe Fenster in den eleganten Suiten geben den Blick frei auf den internationalen Yachthafen.

Des portes fenêtres dans les élégantes suites ouvrent la vue sur le port de plaisance international.

Las ventanas hasta el suelo de las elegantes suites permiten ver el puerto internacional de yates.

Finestre con dimensioni dal tetto al pavimento, di cui sono corredate le eleganti suites, danno libera la vista sul porto internazionale degli yacht.

In comfortable armchairs with a view of Table Mountain, guests here enjoy Africa's sunshine and let the day draw to a close.

In gemütlichen Sesseln mit Blick auf den Tafelberg genießen Gäste hier Afrikas Sonne und lassen den Tag ausklingen.

Dans de confortables fauteuils, avec vue sur la Table Mountain, les hôtes profitent du soleil de l'Afrique et savourent la soirée.

En los cómodos sillones con vistas a la meseta, los huéspedes pueden disfrutar del sol de África y del paso de los días.

In comode poltrone con vista sulla Table Mountain gli ospiti godono il sole africano e attendono che si faccia sera.

Mount Nelson Hotel

Cape Town, South Africa

At the foot of Table Mountain, Cape Town's landmark, the well up to a century-old hotel is located here. The hotel itself is a legend. After extensive renovations the "Pink Lady" as guests affectionately call the hotel because of its pink facade, can receive its guests again with a quite special colonial charm. The 201 rooms and suites are distributed around the main building and the restored historical summerhouses in the park, measuring 3 hectares and originally planted in 1843. The park still has its valuable and original stock of old trees.

Am Fuße des Tafelbergs, des Wahrzeichen Kapstadts, gelegen ist das gut hundert Jahre alte Hotel selbst eine Legende. Nach umfangreicher Renovierung kann die „Pink Lady", wie die Gäste das Hotel wegen seiner rosaroten Fassade liebevoll nennen, wieder mit einem ganz besonderen kolonialen Charme aufwarten. Die 201 Zimmer und Suiten verteilen sich auf das Hauptgebäude und die restaurierten historischen Gartenhäuser im schon 1843 angelegten, drei Hektar großen Park mit seinem wertvollen alten Baumbestand.

Au pied de la Table Mountain, l'emblème de Cape Town, cet hôtel largement centenaire est une véritable légende. Après une importante réfection, la « Dame Rose », comme le surnomment gentiment ses hôtes en raison de sa façade rose, peut de nouveau se présenter avec un charme colonial tout particulier. Les 201 chambres et suites se répartissent sur le bâtiment principal et les maisons de jardin historiques restaurées, dans un parc de trois hectares aménagé dès 1843 et planté de vieux arbres précieux.

A los pies de la meseta, el símbolo de la Ciudad del Cabo, se encuentra este centenario hotel, toda una leyenda. Después de profundas reformas, el "Pink Lady", como le llaman con cariño sus huéspedes por su fachada rosa, ha recuperado su especial encanto colonial. Las 201 habitaciones y suites están ubicadas en el edificio principal, y los históricos pabellones, levantados en 1843 y actualmente restaurados, se reparten por el jardín de tres hectáreas con viejos y valiosos árboles.

Ai piedi della Table Mountain, il simbolo di Città del Capo, è ubicato l'Hotel che esiste da ben cento anni, tanto da essere anch'esso una leggenda. La "Pink Lady", come viene chiamato dagli ospiti amorevolmente per la sua facciata color rosa, può presentarsi di nuovo nel suo fascino coloniale tutto particolare dopo essere stato restaurato da capo a fondo. Le 201 camere e suites si suddividono fra l'edificio principale ed i padiglioni storici nel parco di tre ettari realizzato già nel 1843 e dal pregiato e antico patrimonio arboreo.

In the freshly renovated tea lounge, the best afternoon tea is served outside of the British Isles.

In der frisch renovierten Tea-Lounge wird der beste Afternoon-Tea jenseits der britischen Inseln serviert.

Dans le salon de thé fraîchement rénové on boit le meilleur thé de l'après-midi servi hors des îles britanniques.

En el salón de té recién renovado se sirve el mejor té de las cinco fuera de la isla británica.

Nella Tea-Lounge, da poco rinnovata, viene servito il miglior „Afternoon-Tea" al di fuori delle Isole Britanniche.

The newly opened Planet Champagne Bar by the South African designer Graham Viney quickly advanced to Cape Town's "place to be".

Die neu eröffnete Planet Champagne Bar des südafrikanischen Designers Graham Viney avancierte schnell zum „Place to be" in Kapstadt.

Le bar Planet Champagne du concepteur sud-africain Graham Viney qui a récemment ouvert ses portes est vite devenu le dernier « lieu à la mode » de Cape Town.

El recién inaugurado Planet Champagne Bar, del diseñador sudafricano Graham Viney, se ha convertido en poco tiempo en una de las mejores direcciones de la Ciudad del Cabo.

Il bar Planet Champagne Bar, aperto da poco e ideato dal designer sudafricano Graham Viney, è presto avanzato a "Place to be" quale posto di ritrovo per eccellenza a Città del Capo.

The Twelve Apostles Hotel & Spa

Cape Town, South Africa

In front of your door is the blue and shimmering Atlantic Ocean, behind the hotel is the majestic Table Mountain: the Twelve Apostles Hotel & Spa is located in one of South Africa's most beautiful spots and only 10 minutes from Cape Town's city center. Amidst cinematic views, guests will find rooms here in classically elegant understatement, creative Cape cuisine and a real dream of a fitness area, which won the award of "Leading Spa 2005".

Vor der Tür der blau glitzernde Atlantik, hinter dem Haus der majestätische Tafelberg: Das Twelve Apostles Hotel & Spa liegt an einem der schönsten Plätze Südafrikas und gerade einmal zehn Minuten vom Zentrum Kapstadts entfernt. Neben kinotauglichen Aussichten warten hier Zimmer in klassisch-elegantem Understatement, kreative Kap-Küche und ein traumhafter Wellnessbereich, der als „Leading Spa 2005" ausgezeichnet wurde.

Face au bleu scintillant de l'Atlantique, à l'arrière de la maison, la majestueuse Table Mountain : le Twelve Apostles Hotel & Spa se situe à l'un des endroits les plus beaux d'Afrique du Sud, juste à dix minutes du centre ville de Cape Town. Dans un décor de carte postale, on découvre ici des chambres au charme classique et discret, une cuisine du Cap inventive et un espace de fitness de rêve désigné « Spa Leader 2005 ».

Ante la puerta, el brillante Atlántico, detrás de la casa, la majestuosa meseta: el Twelve Apostles Hotel & Spa está situado en uno de los lugares más bellos de Sudáfrica y a tan sólo diez minutos del centro de la Ciudad del Cabo. Además de unas vistas de película, al visitante le esperan aquí habitaciones de clásica elegancia, una cocina creativa y un balneario de ensueño premiado con el "Leading Spa 2005".

Davanti alla porta l'Oceano Atlantico che luccica, dietra alla casa la maestosa Table Mountain: l'albergo Twelve Apostles Hotel & Spa con il suo centro benessere è ubicato in uno dei posti più belli del Sud Africa e distante dal centro di Città del Capo soli dieci minuti. Oltre a panorami da cinema, ci sono qui camere in classico elegante understatement, cucina creativa e un ambito wellness, premiato quale „Leading SPA 2005", ad attendere gli ospiti.

From many of the 55 rooms and 15 suites, you look directly onto the Atlantic waves. All rooms are individually furnished—for example, in nautical stripes or African nature look.

Von vielen der 55 Zimmer und 15 Suiten aus blickt man direkt auf die Wellen des Atlantiks. Alle Räume sind individuell eingerichtet – zum Beispiel in maritimem Streifendesign oder in afrikanischem Naturlook.

Nombre des 55 chambres et des 15 suites donnent directement sur les vagues de l'Atlantique. Toutes bénéficient d'une décoration individuelle – par exemple le motif marin à rayures ou l'aspect africain naturel.

Desde muchas de sus 55 habitaciones y 15 suites se disfruta de la vista sobre las olas del Atlántico. Todas las habitaciones han sido individual-mente decoradas, por ejemplo, en el típico diseño marítimo a rayas o en un natural estilo africano.

Da molte delle 55 camere e 15 suites si guarda direttamente sulle onde dell'Atlantico. Tutti gli ambienti sono arredati in modo singolare – per esempio con un design marino a righe o nel naturale look africano.

By the fireside in the Leopard Bar you can relax; and that also applies to the two restaurants and the award-winning spa. The hotel is located exactly between the ocean and the mountains.

Am Kamin der Leopard Bar kann man entspannen; ebenso wie in den zwei Restaurants sowie dem preisgekrönten Spa. Das Hotel liegt genau zwischen dem Ozean und den Bergen.

Près de la cheminée du Leopard Bar on peut se détendre ; ainsi que dans les deux restaurants et le Spa qui a reçu un prix. L'hôtel se trouve exactement entre l'océan et les montagnes.

El huésped puede relajarse delante de la chimenea del Leopard Bar, en los dos restaurantes en el premiado balneario. El hotel está situado justo entre el océano y la montaña.

Davanti al camino di Leopard Bar ci si può tranquillamente rilassare; come pure nei due ristoranti e nella SPA premiata. L'albergo è ubicato esattamente fra l'oceano e le montagne.

The Twelve Apostles Hotel & Spa *Cape Town, South Africa*   149

Birkenhead House

Hermanus, South Africa

Lucent as the crests of waves, the hotel rises from a cliff above "Walker Bay". Light, shell tones influence the interior with nostalgic baths, antiques and chaise-longues that you leave at the most to take a refreshing dip in one of the three pools and on the beautiful bathing beach. From the terrace, guests can watch the Southern Right whales, which come into the bay to calf. In the evening, when the lanterns are lit on the patio and the sea air circulates in the dining room, the young hotel team serves freshly caught fish, lobster and sushi.

Leuchtend wie die Schaumkronen der Wellen erhebt sich das Hotel auf einem Felsen über der „Walker-Bay". Helle Muscheltöne prägen auch das Interieur mit nostalgischen Bädern, Antiquitäten und Chaiselonguen, die man höchstens verlässt, um sich in einem der drei Pools und am schönen Badestrand zu erfrischen. Von der Terrasse aus können Gäste Southern Right Wale beobachten, die zum Kalben in die Bucht kommen. Abends, wenn die Laternen im Patio leuchten und Meeresluft in den Speisesaal weht, serviert das junge Hotelteam fangfrischen Fisch, Hummer und Sushi.

Rayonnant comme la couronne d'écume des vagues, l'hôtel se dresse sur un rocher au-dessus de la « Walker-Bay ». Des tons de coquillage clair caractérisent les intérieurs, avec des salles de bains nostalgiques, des antiquités et des chaises longues que l'on ne quitte que pour aller se rafraîchir dans une des trois piscines ou sur la magnifique plage. De la terrasse, les hôtes peuvent observer la baleine australe venue mettre bas dans la baie. Le soir, quand les lanternes s'allument dans le patio et qu'une brise marine souffle dans la salle à manger, la jeune équipe de l'hôtel sert des poissons fraîchement pêchés, du homard et du sushi.

Este hotel, luciente como la espuma de las crestas de las olas, se levanta en la roca por encima de la "Walker-Bay". Los colores claros de las conchas impregnan el interior, con cuartos de baños nostálgicos, antigüedades y sillones chaise longue que el visitante sólo abandonará para refrescarse en una de las tres piscinas o en la playa. Desde la terraza, los huéspedes pueden observar a las ballenas Southern Right, que se dirigen a las bahías a parir. Por la tarde, cuando las farolas del patio se iluminan y el aire del mar recorre el comedor, el joven equipo del hotel sirve el pescado y las langostas recién pescados y el sushi.

Luminosa come la schiuma sulle onde si eleva l'albergo su una roccia sopra la "Walker-Bay". Chiari toni dei colori delle conchiglie danno la loro impronta anche agli ambienti all'interno: i bagni dal sapore d'antico per i nostalgici, antichità e chaise longue che si abbandonano solo per rinfrescarsi en una delle tre piscine o alla bella spiaggia. Dalla terrazza gli ospiti possono osservare le balene della specie Southern right che vengono nella baia per figliare. La sera, quando sono accese le lanterne nel patio e la brezza del mare aleggia nella sala da pranzo, il giovane team dell'albergo serve pesce appena preso, astici e sushi.

Take a dive,—guests can dive in the pool and in the sheltered bay that stretches right in front of the hotel.

Abtauchen können Gäste im Pool und in der geschützten Bucht, die sich gleich vor dem Hotel erstreckt.

Les hôtes peuvent plonger dans la piscine ou dans la baie protégée qui s'étend juste devant l'hotel.

Los huéspedes pueden bañarse en la piscina y en la bahía protegida que se extiende delante de este hotel.

Immergere si possono gli ospiti nella piscina e nella baia protetta, che si estende direttamente davanti al hotel.

Instant relaxation *is guaranteed by sun-loungers on the veranda and the comfortable four-posters in the suites.*

Sofortige Entspannung *garantieren Sonnenliegen auf der Veranda und die komfortablen Himmelbetten der Suiten.*

La détente immédiate *est garantie par les bains de soleil sur la véranda et dans les confortables lits à baldaquin des suites.*

Las tumbonas *de la terraza acristalada y las cómodas camas con dosel de las suites, garantizan la relajación inmediata.*

Distensione immediata *garantiscono le sdraio sulla veranda ed i comodi letti a baldacchino delle suites.*

Tone on tone colored classical divans, nostalgic bathtubs and modern washing basins perfectly harmonize with each other.

Ton in Ton gehaltene antike Rekamieren, nostalgische Badewannen und moderne Waschbecken harmonieren perfekt miteinander.

D'antiques divans ton sur ton, de nostalgiques baignoires et des lavabos modernes se côtoient en parfaite harmonie.

Antiguos divanes conservados tono sobre tono, bañeras nostálgicas y modernos lavabos armonizan perfectamente entre sí.

Tono su tono sono tenute antiche recamiere, bagni dal sapore d'antico e lavandini moderni armonizzano perfettamente fra di loro.

Grootbos Nature Reserve

Hermanus Gansbaai, South Africa

Here it is a success: the optimal combination of luxury and environmental protection. The clear, sober furnishing in the houses is in contrast to the luscious Fynbos vegetation, which grows up in front of the windows. This is regarded as one of the six botanical wonders of the world and stretches to the dunes and cliffs of Walker Bay, where whales and seals play around. Guests at Micheal and Tertius Lutzeyer's place find a real paradise, which invites you to stay because of the fine cuisine, comfortable bar and 23 suites of Garden and Forest Lodge.

Hier ist sie gelungen: die optimale Verbindung von Luxus und Naturschutz. Die klare, sachliche Einrichtung der Häuser, steht im Kontrast zur üppigen Fynbos-Vegetation, die sich vor den Fenstern ausbreitet. Sie gilt als eines der sechs botanischen Wunder dieser Erde und reicht bis zu den Dünen und Klippen der Walker Bay, wo sich Wale und Robben tummeln. Gäste finden bei Michael und Tertius Lutzeyer ein wahres Paradies, das mit feiner Küche, gemütlicher Bar und den 23 Suiten der Garden- und Forest Lodge zum Bleiben einlädt.

Voilà une parfaite réussite : l'association idéale du luxe et de l'écologie. L'aménagement clair et fonctionnel des maisons contraste avec l'opulence de la végétation du fynbos qui s'étend sous les fenêtres. Celle-ci, considérée comme l'une des six merveilles botaniques de la terre, s'étend jusqu'aux dunes et aux rochers de la Walker Bay où s'ébattent baleines et phoques. Les hôtes découvrent chez Michael et Tertius Lutzeyer un véritable paradis où l'on souhaiterait rester pour sa cuisine fine, son bar confortable et les 23 suites du Garden et Forest Lodge.

Aquí se ha conseguido unir de forma óptima el lujo con la protección de la naturaleza. La clara y sencilla decoración de las casas contrasta con el fynbos, la exuberante vegetación arbustiva de la zona, que se extiende delante de las ventanas. El fynbos se cuenta entre las seis maravillas botánicas del mundo y llega hasta las dunas y los arrecifes de la Walker Bay, donde nadan las ballenas y las focas. Los huéspedes encuentran en este hotel de Michael y Tertius Lutzeyer un verdadero paraíso que invita a quedarse, con su deliciosa cocina, su agradable bar y las 23 suites de las casas Garden y Forest.

Qui è riuscita: l'unione ottimale fra lusso e tutela della natura. L'arredamento realistico e schietto delle case sta in contrasto con la rigogliosa vegetazione fynbos, che si estende davanti alle finestre. È considerata una delle sei meraviglie botaniche di questo mondo e va fino alle dune e alla scogliera della Walker Bay, dove scorrazzano balene e foche. Gli ospiti trovano da Michael e Tertius Lutzeyer un vero paradiso, che con la buona cucina, un bar accogliente e le 23 suites del Garden- e Forest Lodge invita a rimanere.

Lots of glass lets your gaze roam unhindered out to nature that is brought indoors by decorative ostrich eggs and photos of exotic flowers.

Viel Glas lässt die Blicke ungehindert in die Natur schweifen, ins Haus geholt wird sie durch dekorative Straußeneier und Fotografien exotischer Blüten.

A travers de nombreuses vitres les regards contemplent la nature sans obstacle ; à l'intérieur elle est présente sous forme de décoratifs œufs d'autruche et de photos de fleurs exotiques.

La gran cantidad de cristal permite la vista sin obstáculos de la naturaleza, que continúa en la casa a través de los decorativos huevos de avestruz y las fotografías de exóticas flores.

Tanto vetro lascia vagare lo sguardo sulla natura senza impedimento alcuno: natura che si può portare in casa sotto forma di decorative uova di struzzo e fotografie di fiori esotici.

The spacious pool reflects the blue of the sky; the warm colors of the African soil are repeated in the interior.

Der großzügige Pool reflektiert das Blau des Himmels, die warmen Farben der afrikanischen Erde finden sich im Interieur wieder.

La grande piscine reflète le bleu du ciel ; les chaudes couleurs de la terre africaine se retrouvent à l'intérieur.

La gran piscina refleja el azul del cielo y los cálidos colores de la tierra africana se extienden hasta el interior.

L'ampia piscina riflette l'azzurro del cielo. I colori caldi della terra africana si ritrovano negli ambienti interni.

If nature, *like here on the terrace, is integrated rather than destroyed, you can enjoy a peaceful sleep with a clear conscience.*

Wird die Natur, *wie hier auf der Terrasse, umbaut anstatt zerstört, lässt es sich ruhigen Gewissens himmlisch schlafen.*

Quand la *construction, comme ici sur la terrasse, s'intègre à la nature au lieu de la détruire, on peut dormir divinement en toute quiétude.*

Si en vez de *destruir la naturaleza se construye integrándola, como en esta terraza, es posible dormir plácidamente con la conciencia tranquila.*

Quando la natura, *anziché essere distrutta, viene inclusa — come qui sulla terrazza — costruendovi intorno, si può dormire divinamente colla coscienza tranquilla.*

Sanbona Wildlife Reserve

Little Karoo, South Africa

Only three hours away from Cape Town, at the foot of the bizarrely shaped Warmwaterberg,—this is the location of Tilney Manor and Khanni Lodge, two idyllic summer houses built in Dutch Cape style. Freestanding bathtubs, rooms with open fires, a fitness area and colors that harmonize with the tones of the surrounding stones and plants make the lodge an ideal relaxation spot in the wilderness. In Khanni Lodge, swing doors open onto the pool and water hole. Most frequent guest: Eland antelopes.

Nur drei Stunden von Kapstadt entfernt, am Fuße des bizarr geformten Warmwaterberg, liegen Tilney Manor und Khanni Lodge, zwei idyllische Sommerhäuser im kapholländischen Stil. Freistehende Badewannen, Kaminzimmer, ein Wellnessbereich und Farben, die mit den Tönen der Steine und Pflanzen der Umgebung harmonieren, machen die Lodge zum idealen Erholungsort in der Wildniss. In der Khanni Lodge öffnen sich Flügeltüren zu Pool und Wasserloch. Häufigster Gast: Eland-Antilopen.

A seulement trois heures de Cape Town, au pied du « Warmwaterberg » aux formes bizarres, se trouvent deux villas idylliques, Tilney Manor et Khanni Lodge, réalisées dans le style hollandais du cap. Des baignoires en plein air, des chambres avec cheminée, un espace de fitness et des couleurs en harmonie avec les tons des pierres et des plantes environnantes font de ce lodge un lieu de détente idéal dans le désert. Dans le Khanni Lodge, les portes fenêtres s'ouvrent sur la piscine et le point d'eau. L'hôte le plus assidu : l'antilope éland.

A sólo tres horas de Ciudad del Cabo y a los pies de la extraña "Warmwaterberg", se encuentran los lodges Tilney Manor y Khanni, dos idílicas casas de verano de estilo afrikaans. El lodge se convierte en un lugar ideal para el descanso con sus bañeras a cielo raso, las habitaciones con chimenea, un balneario y colores en armonía con los tonos de las piedras y las plantas del entorno. En el lodge Khanni las puertas batientes se abren a la piscina y a la laguna. El huésped más habitual: el antílope Eland.

Soltanto tre ore lontane da Città del Capo, ai piedi della "Warmwaterberg" dalla forma bizzarra, sono ubicate due case estive idilliche nello stile afrikaans. Vasche da bagno all'aperto, camera con camino, un centro benessere e colori che armonizzano con i toni delle pietre e delle piante dei dintorni, fanno di queste lodge il luogo riposo ideale nel deserto. Nel lodge Khanni si aprono porte a battenti per l'accesso alla piscina e alla buca d'acqua. Ospiti frequenti: antilopi eland.

Tilney Manor with its six spacious suites is built in typical Dutch Cape style.

Tilney Manor mit seinen sechs großzügigen Suiten ist im typisch kapholländischen Stil erbaut.

Tilney Manor qui comprend six suites spacieuses est construit dans le style hollandais du cap typique.

Tilney Manor con sus seis amplias suites ha sico construido según el típico estilo afrikaans.

Tilney Manor con le sue sei ampie suites è costruito nel tipico stile afrikaans.

Chic, dignified and inhabitable: the interior of both lodges. You can hardly believe that elephants, lions and rhinoceros live right nearby.

Chic, gediegen und wohnlich ist das Interieur der beiden Lodges. Kaum zu glauben, dass in unmittelbarer Nähe Elefant, Löwe und Nashorn leben.

Chic, pur et confortable peuvent qualifier l'intérieur des deux lodges. Difficile de croire qu'à proximité immédiate vivent des lions, des éléphants et des rhinocéros.

El interior de ambas instalaciones es elegante, sencillo y acogedor. Resulta casi imposible de creer que cerca de allí vivan elefantes, leones y rinocerontes.

Chic, curato e confortevole è l'interno dei due lodge: tanto che è difficile credere che nelle immediate vicinanze vivano elefanti, leoni e rinoceronti.

The Plettenberg

Plettenberg Bay, South Africa

The location on the "Look-out Rock" directly on the Indian Ocean, with a view of the Tsitsikamma Mountains, guarantees a fantastic view. Designed as a beach hotel, "The Plett", as fans affectionately call it, is surrounded by sun, sand and sea. This light expanse is continued in the 36 rooms or suites and two villas. A decidedly young and light style is carried through the entire hotel, whose excellent cuisine is complimented by a state-of-the-art wine cellar.

Die Lage auf den „Look-out Rock" direkt am Indischen Ozean, mit Blick auf die Tsitsikamma Berge, garantiert eine tolle Aussicht. Als Strandhotel konzipiert, umgibt sich „The Plett", wie es von Fans liebevoll genannt wird, mit Sonne, Sand und Meer. Diese lichte Weite setzt sich in 36 Zimmern bzw. Suiten und zwei Villen fort. Ein betont junger und leichter Stil zieht sich durch das ganze Hotel, dessen ausgezeichnete Küche durch einen state-of-the-art Weinkeller ergänzt wird.

Sa situation exceptionnelle sur le « Look-out Rock » garantit une vue imprenable sur l'océan indien et les monts Tsitsikamma. Conçu comme un établissement de bains, cet hôtel gentiment surnommé « The Plett » par ses fans, est entouré de soleil, de sable et de mer. Les 36 chambres et suites des deux villas offrent ce paysage lumineux. Un style résolument jeune et simple caractérise tout l'hôtel dont l'excellente cuisine est accompagnée par une cave à vins à la hauteur de son standing.

Su situación sobre el "Look-out Rock" a orillas del Océano Índico, con vistas a las montañas Tsitsikamma, garantiza un paisaje espectacular. Concebido como un hotel de la playa, el "The Plett", como le llaman con cariño sus fans, está rodeado de sol, arena y playa. Esta luminosa amplitud continúa en las 36 habitaciones, en las suites y en las dos villas. Un estilo marcadamente joven y ligero está presente en todo el hotel. Su extraordinaria cocina se complementa con una excelente bodega.

La posizione sulla "Look-out Rock" direttamente sull'oceano indiano con vista sui monti del Tsitsikamma garantisce un panorama mozzafiato. Concepito come hotel alla spiaggia "The Plett", come lo chiamano amichevolmente i fans, è circondato da sole, sabbia e mare. Questa luminosa ampiezza continua a sussistere nelle 36 camere o suites e nelle due ville. Uno stile marcatamente giovane e agile si estende attraverso tutto l'albergo, la cui ottima cucina è completata da una cantina di vini state-of-the-art.

Looking out of the windows of the light and individually designed rooms, you sometimes see the waterspouts of whales and dolphins swimming past.

Beim Blick aus den Fenstern der hellen und individuell gestalteten Zimmer sieht man manchmal Wale und Delfine vorbeiprusten.

En regardant par les fenêtres des chambres claires à la décoration individuelle on observe baleines et dauphins s'ébrouant dans la baie.

Desde las ventanas de las luminosas habitaciones, decoradas de forma individual, se pueden ver de vez en cuando a las ballenas y los delfines resoplando.

Guardando fuori dalla finestra delle camere chiare e individuali si vedono a volte passare soffiando le balene ed i delfini.

Inviting and comfortable is how the hotel appears in the evening, when the glow of lamps and candles bathes the fresh colors in a warm light.

Einladend und gemütlich wirkt das Hotel am Abend, wenn der Schein von Lampen und Kerzen die frischen Farben in ein warmes Licht taucht.

Le soir l'hôtel est particulièrement séduisant et confortable quand la lueur des lampes et des bougies plonge ses couleurs fraîches dans une chaude lumière.

Al atardecer, cuando la luz de las lámparas y de las velas sumerge los frescos colores en una cálida luz, el hotel resulta acogedor y agradable.

Invitante e accogliente quando la sera il bagliore delle lampade e delle candele avvolge i freschi colori dell'albergo nella calda luce.

Pastel tones define the design of the communal rooms, while the turquoise-colored water of the pool seems to flow into the deep blue of the ocean.

Pastelltöne bestimmen die Gestaltung der Aufenthaltsräume, während das türkisfarbene Wasser des Pools in das tiefe Blau des Ozeans zu fließen scheint.

Les tons pastel dominent dans la conception des salons tandis que le bleu turquoise de la piscine semble se fondre dans le bleu profond de l'océan.

Los tonos pastel determinan el diseño de los espacios públicos, mientras que el color turquesa del agua de la piscina parece fluir en el azul profundo del océano.

Toni pastello sono dominanti negli ambienti da soggiorno, mentre l'acqua turchese della piscina sembra fluire nell'azzurro intenso dell'oceano.

Tsala Treetop Lodge

Plettenberg Bay, South Africa

Anyone taking a holiday here means to aim high, as the lodge is hidden under the treetops of indigenous forest giants on the Garden Route. This is how a symphony of wood, natural stone and glass was created in the lofty heights near the Tsitsikamma Mountains. Wooden bridges meander through the treetops and connect the lodge's main building with the suites, which are reminiscent of rustic barracks with their quarried stonewalls. Local artists have decorated them with antique textiles and carvings. Magical moments are created, if you watch the forest birds when you swim in the private pool.

Wer hier Urlaub macht, will hoch hinaus, denn die Lodge versteckt sich unter den Wipfel alter Urwaldriesen an der Garden Route. Nahe der Tsitsikamma-Berge entstand so in luftiger Höhe eine Symphonie aus Holz, Naturstein und Glas. Holzstege mäandern durch Baumkronen und verbinden das Haupthaus der Lodge mit den Suiten, die mit ihren Bruchsteinmauern an rustikale Blockhütten erinnern. Lokale Künstler haben sie mit antiken Textilien und Schnitzereien dekoriert. Magische Momente entstehen, wenn man bei einem Bad im Privat-Pool die Vögel des Waldes beobachtet.

Quiconque souhaite passer ses vacances ici doit prendre de l'altitude, car le lodge se cache sous la cime de géants tropicaux sur la Garden Route. Dans les hauteurs aérées des monts Tsitsikamma s'élève une symphonie de bois, pierre et verre. Des passerelles de bois serpentent entre les cimes, reliant le lodge central aux suites qui ressemblent à des cabanes en rondins avec leurs murs de moellons. Des artistes locaux les ont décorés de textiles antiques et de sculptures. Se relaxer dans un bain de sa piscine privée en observant les oiseaux de la forêt est un instant magique.

Quien desee pasar aquí las vacaciones, tiene que querer escalar alto, y es que el hotel se oculta bajo las copas de los árboles gigantes de la selva virgen en la Garden Route. Cerca de las montañas Tsitsikamma, a gran altura, se construyó una sinfonía de madera, piedra y cristal. Pasarelas de madera recorren las copas de los árboles y unen el edificio principal con las suites que, con sus muros de piedra de mampostería, recuerdan a las pequeñas cabañas rústicas. Artistas locales han decorado las habitaciones con antiguos tejidos y tallas de madera. Surge la magia cuando durante el baño en la piscina privada es posible observar a los pájaros de la selva.

Chi fa vacanza qui vuole andare in alto, perchè il lodge si nasconde sotto le cime di vecchi giganti della foresta vergine sulla Garden Route. Vicino ai monti del Tsitsikamma sorse così in ariosa altitudine una sinfonia di legno, pietra naturale e vetro. Passerelle in legno serpeggiano fra le chiome degli alberi e collegano la struttura centrale del lodge con le suites, che con le loro mura in pietra di cava fanno pensare a rusticali case in legno. Momenti magici seguono quando, immersi nell'acqua della piscina privata, si osservano gli uccelli del bosco.

Amongst treetops of ancient trees the intimate lodge is hidden away. Despite its seclusion, it offers maximum luxury. Every suite has a mini pool on the sun deck.

Zwischen den Wipfeln uralter Bäume versteckt sich die intime Lodge. Trotz der Abgeschiedenheit bietet sie größten Luxus. Jede Suite hat einen Mini-Pool auf dem Sonnendeck.

Entre les cimes d'arbres centenaires se cache ce refuge intime. Malgré son isolement il offre un luxe extrême. Chaque suite est dotée d'un mini bassin sur une terrasse.

Este íntimo lodge se oculta entre las copas de los milenarios árboles. A pesar de su situación no se renuncia al lujo. Cada suite dispone de una minipiscina privada en la terraza del tejado.

Fra le cime di alberi antichissimi si nasconde l'accogliente lodge. Nonostante sia così appartato, offre grande lusso. Ogni suite ha una minipiscina nella parte esposta al sole.

Art craftsmen have decorated the suites with carvings, lights out of Kudu antelope horns and gourds.

Kunsthandwerker haben die Suiten mit Schnitzereien, Leuchten aus Kudu-Hörnern und Kalebassen dekoriert.

Des artisans d'art ont décoré toutes les suites avec des sculptures, des lampes en corne de koudou et des calebasses.

Los artesanos han decorado las suites con tallas de madera, lámparas de cuernos de kudu y calabazas.

Artigiani hanno decorato con arte le suites con sculture in legno, lampade di corna di kudu e di baobab.

Behind the hand-carved swing doors the original and romantic lodge provides an excellent South African cuisine and suitable wines.

Hinter den handgeschnitzten Flügeltüren bietet die urig-romantische Lodge hervorragende südafrikanische Küche mit passenden Weinen.

Derrière les portes fenêtres sculptées à la main, ce lodge pittoresque et romantique propose une excellente cuisine sud-africaine arrosée de vins succulents.

Detrás de las puertas batientes hechas a mano, el rústico y romántico hotel ofrece una excelente cocina sudafricana con una buena combinación de vinos.

Dietro alle porte a battenti il lodge originale e romantico offre un'ottima cucina sudafricana insieme al vino adatto.

Tsala Treetop Lodge *Plettenberg Bay, South Africa*   177

The Grace

Johannesburg, South Africa

A fine London Club,—this is what the family-run hotel is like. The hotel is located in the heart of the popular Rosebank quarter, a secure and green suburb. The English style is unmistakable here: floral brocade fabrics, wood paneling, comfortable library, paintings with lavish gold frames, and homemade baking with tea at five o'clock. Incidentally, the best place to take tea is on the roof terrace beneath an African sky and far away from Johannesburg's city bustle.

Einem feinen Londoner Club ähnelt die familiengeleitete Residenz im Herzen des angesagten Viertels Rosebank, einem sicheren, grünen Vorort. Der englische Stil ist hier unverkennbar: Florale Brokatstoffe, Holzvertäfelungen, behagliche Bibliothek, Gemälde mit üppigen Goldrahmen und hausgemachtes Gebäck zum Five o'clock tea. Den genießt man übrigens am besten auf der Dachterrasse unter afrikanischem Himmel, weit ab vom Großstadttrubel Johannesburgs.

Cette résidence ressemblant à un élégant club londonien et dirigée par la famille propriétaire se situe au cœur du quartier très stylé de Rosebank, une banlieue sûre et verdoyante. Le style se traduit ici par une élégance très anglaise: étoffes de brocart à motif floral, lambris de bois, agréable bibliothèque, tableaux aux lourds cadres dorés et petits fours maison pour le thé de cinq heures. La terrasse sur le toit est d'ailleurs l'endroit idéal pour le savourer, sous le ciel africain, loin du tumulte de la grande ville Johannesbourg.

Esta residencia de dirección familiar y que recuerda a un elegante club londinés, está situada en el corazón del barrio más de moda, el Rosebank, un suburbio seguro y verde. Aquí, el estilo inglés es inconfundible: telas brocadas con estampados florales, artesonados de madera, una agradable biblioteca, cuadros con ricos marcos dorados y pastel casero para el té de las cinco. La mejor forma de disfrutarlo es en la terraza de la azotea, bajo el cielo africano, lejos del tumulto de Johannesburgo.

A un eletto club londinese somiglia il complesso a gestione familiare nel cuore del quartiere residenziale di Rosebank, un verde sobborgo tranquillo e sicuro. Lo stile inglese è qui inconfondibile: stoffe in broccato in stile floreale, rivestimenti in legno, biblioteca accogliente, dipinti con ricche cornici dorate e biscotti fatti in casa per il five o'clock tea. Lo si gusta meglio sulla terrazza sul tetto sotto il cielo africano, lontani dal trambusto metropolitano della città di Johannesburg.

After a tour of the district's boutiques, you can relax by browsing, drinking tea and dreaming in the rose-petal bed.

Nach einer Tour durch die Boutiquen des Viertels entspannt man beim Schmökern, Teetrinken und Träumen im Rosenblüten-Bett.

Après une ballade dans les boutiques du quartier on se détend en bouquinant, en buvant un thé et en rêvant dans un lit de pétales de roses.

Después de un recorrido por las boutiques del barrio, el huésped puede relajarse leyendo, bebiendo té y soñando en una cama con pétalos de rosa.

Dopo un giro nelle boutique del quartiere ci si rilassa scartabellando libri, bevendo tè o sognando nel letto di fiori di rose.

Lavish floral and chequed fabrics for the beds, chairs and curtains make the big city hotel a haven of tranquility with English country flair.

Üppige Blumen- und Karostoffe für Betten, Sessel und Gardinen machen aus dem Großstadthotel einen Ruhepol mit englischem Country-Flair.

De riches tissus à fleurs et à carreaux pour les lits, les fauteuils et les rideaux font de cet hôtel citadin un îlot de calme dégageant une ambiance de campagne anglaise.

Ricas telas con motivos florales y estampados a cuadros para las camas, los sillones y las cortinas hacen de este hotel urbano un centro del descanso con un estilo rural inglés.

Stoffe con fiori rigogliosi e a quadretti per letti, poltrone e tende fanno dell'albergo metropolitano un'oasi di pace dal country flair inglese.

Saxon

Johannesburg, South Africa

With a unique style mix of African artists' craftsmanship and designer furniture, the Saxon is an impressive sight in the exclusive suburb of Sandhurst. A glass dome that catches the sunlight arches above the stairway in the lobby. Elegant sofas in the piano lounge, library and dining room invite guests to relax, while shady foliage and the pool nestle in fabulous garden facilities. By the way, the Platinum suite is named after Nelson Mandela, who wrote his autobiography "Long walk to freedom" here after his release from prison.

Mit einem einzigartigen Stilmix aus afrikanischem Kunsthandwerk und Designermöbeln beeindruckt das Saxon im exklusiven Vorort Sandhurst. Über dem Treppenaufgang in der Lobby wölbt sich eine Glaskuppel, die das Sonnenlicht einfängt. In der Piano-Lounge, der Bibliothek und dem Speisesaal laden elegante Sofas zum Entspannen ein, während schattige Lauben und der Pool in herrliche Gartenanlagen eingebettet sind. Die Platinum-Suite ist übrigens nach Nelson Mandela benannt, der hier nach der Entlassung aus der Haft seine Autobiografie „Long walk to freedom" schrieb.

Le mélange des styles unique, conjuguant artisanat africain et meubles de designer, est impressionnant au Saxon situé dans Sandhurst, un quartier très exclusif. Au-dessus des escaliers de la réception s'élève un dôme de verre captant le soleil. Dans le salon à musique, la bibliothèque et la salle à manger, d'élégants sofas invitent à la détente, tandis que des tonnelles ombragées et la piscine vous attendent dans de magnifiques jardins. Par ailleurs, la suite Platinum porte le nom de Nelson Mandela puisqu'il y écrivit son autobiographie « Un long chemin vers la liberté » après sa libération.

El Saxon, situado en el exclusivo barrio Sandhurst, impresiona por su excepcional mezcla cultural y sus muebles de diseño. Sobre la escalera del vestíbulo se arquea una cúpula de vidrio que permite el paso de la luz natural. En el salón del piano, la biblioteca y el comedor, los elegantes sofás invitan a relajarse, mientras que los umbríos cenadores y la piscina están integrados en el maravilloso jardín. La suite Platinum lleva el nombre de Nelson Mandela, quien, después de ser puesto en libertad, escribió aquí su autobiografía "El largo camino hacia la libertad".

Con una mescolanza di stili unica nel suo genere fra artigianato artistico africano e mobili design impressiona il Saxon ubicato nell'esclusivo sobborgo di Sandhurst. A copertura delle scale si curva a volta una cupola di vetro che imprigiona la luce del sole. Nel piano-lounge, nella biblioteca e nella sala da pranzo invitano eleganti sofà a rilassarsi e negli impianti meravigliosi dei giardini sono collocate pergole ombrose e piscine. La Platinum-Suite è stata denominata Nelson Mandela, che scrisse qui, dopo il suo rilascio dalla detenzione, la sua autobiografia "Lungo cammino verso la libertà".

Generosity is what influences the hotel garden here, which has the dimensions of a city park, the pool—probably one of the largest hotel pools ever—, the elegant restaurant as well as the suites.

Großzügigkeit prägt hier den Hotelgarten mit den Ausmaßen eines Stadtparks, das Pool — wohl einer der größten Hotelpools überhaupt —, das elegante Restaurant sowie die Suiten.

L'espace caractérise ici les jardins aux dimensions d'un parc municipal, la piscine — sans doute l'une des plus grandes piscines d'hôtel —, l'élégant restaurant ainsi que les suites.

La amplitud es la principal característica del jardín del hotel, con unas medidas similares a las de un parque municipal, de la piscina, una de las mayores, del elegante restaurante y de las suites.

Vastità è il segno evidente del giardino dell'albergo, paragonabile alle dimensioni di un parco cittadino. Come pure la piscina — forse una delle più grandi piscine d'albergo —, l'elegante ristorante e le suites.

For only 26 hotel suites, the lobby appears virtually majestic. Guests can dine, on request, in the romantic niches outdoors. Below: living room in the Mandela Suite.

Für die nur 26 Suiten des Hotels wirkt die Lobby geradezu majestätisch. Speisen kann man auf Wunsch auch in den romantischen Nischen im Freien. Unten: Wohnzimmer der Mandela Suite.

Pour les quelque 26 suites de l'hôtel, la réception est franchement majestueuse. Les repas peuvent également se prendre dans de romantiques niches en plein air. En bas : le salon de la suite Mandela.

El lobby parece casi majestuoso para un hotel de sólo 26 suites. También es posible cenar al aire libre en románticos rincones. Abajo, cuarto de estar de la suite Mandela.

Per le sole 26 suites dell'albergo la lobby sembra essere addirittura imponente. Su desiderio si può anche mangiare nelle nicchie romantiche all'aria aperta. Sotto: camera di soggiorno della suite Mandela.

Like a lake: the pool extends in front of the wooden swing doors of the spacious suites. An ideal place to escape the hectic bustle of city life.

Wie ein See breitet sich der Pool vor den hölzernen Flügeltüren der weiträumigen Suiten aus. Ein idealer Platz, um der Hektik des Stadtlebens zu entkommen.

Tel un lac, la piscine miroite devant les portes fenêtres en bois des suites spacieuses. Un endroit idéal pour échapper à l'agitation de la vie citadine.

La piscina se extiende como un lago ante las puertas batientes de madera de las amplias suites. El lugar ideal para huir del ajetreo de la vida en la ciudad.

Come un lago si estende la piscina davanti alle porte a battenti in legno delle ampie suites. Un posto ideale per sfuggire all'agitazione febbrile della vita di città.

The Westcliff

Johannesburg, South Africa

Like a Mediterranean village, the luxury hotel with its terraces and balconies clings to a hillside and offers a view of the green Magalies mountains. Cobblestone paths lead to the restaurant and panoramic terrace. Anyone who looks down discovers the elephants in the zoo that is located beneath. The famous South African designer Graham Viney designed the 115 rooms and suites. Lavish floral designs, soft chintz and warm cappuccino tones take care of comfort. The wood-paneled polo lounge quickly advanced to a rendezvous for high society.

Wie ein mediterranes Dorf schmiegt sich das Luxushotel mit seinen Terrassen und Balkonen an einen Hügel mit Blick auf die grünen Magaliesberge. Zu Restaurant und Panoramaterrasse führen Wege aus Pflastersteinen. Wer nach unten schaut, entdeckt Elefanten im darunter liegenden Zoo. Die 115 Zimmer und Suiten hat der bekannte südafrikanische Designer Graham Viney gestaltet. Üppige Blumenmuster, weicher Chintz und warme Cappuccino-Töne sorgen für Behaglichkeit. Die holzgetäfelte Polo Lounge avancierte schnell zu einem Treffpunkt der High Society.

Tel un village méditerranéen, cet hôtel de luxe avec ses terrasses et balcons s'adosse à une colline, offrant une belle vue sur les vertes montagnes de la Magalies. Des chemins pavés conduisent au restaurant et à la terrasse panoramique. En regardant vers le bas, on découvre les éléphants du zoo situé en contrebas. C'est le célèbre designer sud-africain Graham Viney, qui a réalisé les 115 chambres et suites. De généreux motifs floraux, du chintz moelleux, des tons chauds de cappuccino créent une impression de bien-être. Le salon Polo aux lambris de bois est vite devenu le point de rencontre de la haute société.

Este hotel de lujo, con sus terrazas y sus balcones, parece un pueblo mediterráneo. Sus casas se agrupan en una colina con vistas a las verdes montañas Magalies. Caminos de adoquín conducen hasta el restaurante y a la terraza panorámica. Si se mira hacia abajo pueden verse los elefantes del zoo. Las 115 habitaciones y suites han sido decoradas por el famoso diseñador sudafricano Graham Viney. Ricos dibujos florales, telas suaves de chintz y colores tostados hacen que las estancias resulten confortables. El salón Polo, revestido de madera, se convirtió rápidamente en el lugar de encuentro de la alta sociedad.

Come un villaggio mediterraneo, l'albergo di lusso con le sue terrazze e balconi si appoggia ai verdi monti Magalies. Vie lastricate conducono al ristorante e alla terrazza panoramica. Chi guarda in giù, scopre elefanti nello zoo sottostante. Le 115 camere e suites sono state ideate dal designer africano molto conosciuto, Graham Viney. Ricchi disegni a fiori, morbido chintz e caldi toni cappuccino danno una sensazione di accoglienza. Il Pololounge, rivestito di legno, è presto diventato un punto d'incontro dell'alta società.

Leather sofas, historic photos, and an open fire: the Polo Lounge is the city's most popular "living room" after a civilized dinner.

Ledersofas, historische Fotos, Kaminfeuer: Die Polo Lounge ist nach einem gepflegten Dinner das angesagteste „Wohnzimmer" der Stadt.

Des sofas de cuir, des photos historiques, un feu de cheminée : le salon Polo est la « salle de séjour » la plus prisée de la ville à la suite d'un dîner raffiné.

Sofás de cuero, fotos históricas, el fuego de la chimenea: después de una deliciosa cena, el salón Polo es el "cuarto de estar" más de moda de la ciudad.

Sofà in pelle, fotografie storiche, fuoco nel camino. La Polo lounge, dopo un dinner scelto, è il "soggiorno" più ricercato della città.

Although in the center of a major city, the hotel resembles more a resort. From the pool, if you are lucky you can even watch elephants, as you look straight out to the site of Johannesburg's Zoo.

Obwohl inmitten der Großstadt wirkt das Hotel eher wie ein Resort. Vom Pool aus kann man mit etwas Glück sogar Elefanten beobachten, denn man blickt geradewegs auf das Gelände des Johannesburger Zoos.

Bien que situé au centre d'une grande ville, l'hôtel fait plutôt penser à un resort. Du bord de la piscine, avec un peu de chance, on peut même observer les éléphants car le regard plonge directement sur les installations du zoo de Johannesbourg.

A pesar de que el hotel parece un complejo hotelero dentro de la metrópoli, desde la piscina se pueden ver con un poco de suerte a los elefantes, porque el hotel está orientado hacia el zoo.

Nonostante si trovi in una grande città, l'albergo sembra piuttosto un resort. Dalla piscina, con un pò di fortuna, si possono persino osservare Elefanti, in quanto si guarda direttamente sull'aera dello zoo di Johannesburg.

Phinda Private Game Reserve

Kwa Zulu Natal, South Africa

Three-for-one: exclusive lodges delight guests in the private wildlife park with comfort and award-winning design. Forest Lodge, built on stilts, is hidden in a rare sand forest. Its style, Zulu-Zen, is unique: minimalist furniture and specially selected Zulu handcrafted art on gleaming wooden floors. Vlei Lodge is located in the middle of wetlands that are heavily populated by birds and the lodge harmonizes with nature. Guests have breathtaking views into the valley from Rock Lodge, which is built on jagged cliffs.

Gleich drei außergewöhnliche Lodges begeistern in dem privaten Wildpark mit Komfort und preisgekröntem Design. Die auf Stelzen errichtete Forest Lodge versteckt sich in einem seltenen Sandwald. Ihr Stil, Zulu-Zen, ist einzigartig: minimalistische Möbel und ausgesuchte Zulu-Handwerkskunst auf glänzenden Holzböden. Die Vlei Lodge liegt inmitten vogelreicher Feuchtwiesen in Einklang mit der Natur. Von der Rock Lodge, die auf schroffen Felsen erbaut ist, hat man atemberaubende Ausblicke ins Tal.

Ce sont trois lodges exceptionnelles qui enthousiasment le voyageur dans ce parc naturel privé par leur confort et leur conception maintes fois couronnée. Le Forest Lodge bâti sur pilotis se niche dans une forêt de sable rare. Son style, « zoulou zen », est unique : meubles minimalistes et artisanat d'art zoulou sur de reluisants parquets. Le Vlei Lodge se situe au milieu d'un site humide plein d'oiseaux en harmonie avec la nature. Le Rock Lodge édifié sur des rochers escarpés procure une vue fabuleuse sur la vallée.

Dentro de la reserva privada de caza, tres extraordinarios edificios entusiasman por su confort y su premiado diseño. El Forest Lodge, situado sobre zancos de madera, se oculta en un bosque de arena poco usual. Su estilo zulú zen es único: muebles minimalistas y escogidas artesanías zulús sobre brillantes suelos de madera. El Vlei Lodge está situado en medio de una pradera húmeda, con una importante población de pájaros, en armonía con la naturaleza. Desde el Rock Lodge, construido sobre escarpadas rocas, se disfruta de unas espectaculares vistas del valle.

Tre lodge, e tutti e tre fuori del comune, entusiasmano nella riserva privata per la loro comodità e per il design premiato. Il Forest Lodge, costruito su palafitte, è nascosto in una rara foresta di sabbia. Il suo stile, Zulu-Zen, è proprio unico: mobili minimalistici e arte artigiana Zulu su lucida pavimentazione in legno. Il Vlei Lodge è ubicato in mezzo a umidi prati, popolati da moltissimi uccelli, in armonia con la natura. Dal Rock Lodge, costruito su rupi erte, si ha una vista mozzafiato sulla valle.

Vlei Lodge has two faces: from the outside, it looks rustic with white-washed walls; from the inside it's Asian and exotic.

Die Vlei Lodge hat zwei Gesichter: Von außen gibt sie sich rustikal mit weißverputzten Mauern, von innen asiatisch-exotisch.

Le Vlei Lodge a deux visages: à l'extérieur il présente un aspect rustique avec ses murs de crépi blanc, à l'intérieur il est asiatico-exotique.

El Vlei Lodge posee dos caras: por fuera rústicos muros blancos y, por dentro, exotismo asiático.

Il Vlei Lodge ha due facce: all'esterno si dà rusticale con mura intonacate di bianco, all'interno è esotico-orientale.

Anyone who takes a refreshing dip in the pool at Rock Lodge has the Leopard rock in sight and guests in the glass structure of Forest Lodge have a view of the tropical forest.

Wer sich im Pool der Rock Lodge erfrischt, hat den Leopardenfelsen im Blick, die Gäste der verglasten Forest Lodge den Tropenwald.

Le voyageur qui se rafraîchit dans la piscine du Rock Lodge admire le rocher aux léopards, le visiteur du Forest Lodge entouré de vitres contemple la forêt tropicale.

Desde la piscina del edificio Rock pueden verse las rocas con manchas de leopardo y, desde el acristalado Forest, el bosque tropical.

Chi si rinfresca nella piscina del Rock Lodge guarda sulla rupe dei leopardi; gli ospiti del Forest Lodge a vetri hanno la vista sulla foresta tropicale.

Singita Lebombo Lodge
Kruger National Park, South Africa

Like eagles nests, the 15 guest lofts in the lodge, located in the middle of Kruger National Park, claw themselves onto the steep incline of the cliff-head. Floor-to-ceiling glass walls give a wide view across the South African Savannah as far as the red cliffs of the Lebombo mountains. Cantilevered white cushioned beds on the sun decks invite you to watch the spectacular color-play of the African sky. Nature plays the main part in the Singita Lebombo Lodge, which is cultivating a new, contemporary safari style.

Adlernestern gleich krallen sich die 15 Gäste-Lofts der mitten im Krüger Nationalpark gelegenen Lodge an den steil abfallenden Felsvorsprung. Raumhohe Glaswände erlauben einen weiten Blick über die südafrikanische Savanne bis hin zu den roten Felsen des Lebombo-Gebirges. Ausladende weiße Polsterbetten auf den Sonnendecks laden dazu ein, das grandiose Farbenspiel des afrikanischen Himmels zu beobachten. Die Natur spielt die Hauptrolle in der Singita Lebombo-Lodge, die einen neuen zeitgemäßen Safari-Stil kultiviert.

Tels des nids d'aigle, les 15 lofts s'agrippent au sommet d'une falaise escarpée au sein du Kruger National Park. Les chambres aux murs de verre donnent sur toute l'étendue de la savane africaine jusqu'aux roches rouges des monts Lebombo. Des canapés blancs installés sur la terrasse invitent à contempler le scintillement grandiose du ciel africain. La nature est maître des lieux dans le Lebombo Lodge qui cultive un nouveau style safari moderne.

Los huéspedes de los 15 lofts situados en medio del parque natural Kruger, se agarran firmemente al suelo cuando se encuentran ante el escarpado precipicio. Las mamparas de las habitaciones permiten disfrutar de una extensa vista de la sabana africana hasta las rocas rojas de las montañas de Lebombo. Las acolchadas tumbonas de la terraza invitan a observar el grandioso juego de colores del cielo africano. La naturaleza es un elemento primordial en el hotel Singita Lebombo, donde se cultiva un nuevo y modero estilo de safari.

Come nidi d'aquila i 15 loft per gli ospiti del lodge ubicato in mezzo al Parco Nazionale Kruger si aggrappano alla sporgenza rocciosa in declivio. Pareti in vetro, alte fino al soffitto, permettono un'ampia vista sulla Savana sudafricana fino alle rosse rocce delle montagne di Lebombo. Larghi letti bianchi imbottiti disposti al sole invitano a osservare il grandioso gioco di colori del cielo africano. La natura gioca il ruolo principale nel lodge Singita Lebombo, che mantiene uno stile safari moderno.

Crafted by hand: wood imitates the material that eagles use to build their nests.

Von Hand bearbeitetes Holz imitiert das Material, mit dem Adler ihre Nester bauen.

Le bois taillé à la main imite le matériau avec lequel les aigles construisent leurs nids.

Esta madera trabajada artesanalmente imita el material con el que las águilas construyen sus nidos.

Legno lavorato a mano imita il materiale con cui le aquile fanno i loro nidi.

In contemporary African design,—this is how the Bush Spa in the Lebombo Village is also created.

In zeitgemäßem afrikanischem Design ist auch der im Lebombo Village gelegene Busch-Spa gestaltet.

Dans un style africain moderne, le Spa de brousse est installé dans le Lebombo Village.

En un moderno estilo africano está diseñado el Bush-Spa situado en el Lebombo Village.

Nel moderno design africano è realizzata anche la Busch-SPA, ubicata direttamente nel Lebombo Village.

From the 40-meter long pool and the open Lobby Bar, a breathtaking view opens up across the Savannah.

Vom 40 Meter langen Pool und der offenen Lobby-Bar aus eröffnet sich ein atemberaubender Blick über die Savanne.

Du bord de la piscine de 40 m de long et du bar en plein air, la vue sur la savane est exceptionnelle.

Desde la piscina de 40 metros de largo y desde el bar del vestíbulo, se abre una espectacular vista sobre la sabana.

Dalla piscina, lunga 40 metri, e dal Lobby-Bar si apre una vista mozzafiato sulla Savana.

Singita Sweni Lodge
Kruger National Park, South Africa

New standards of style and luxury are set by the intimate lodge on Sweni river: glass walls surround six suites, which are designed in soft khaki tones. The effect: the distinctions between loft-style suites and nature merge together. Traditional art carvings, clay pots and batik fabrics contrast with the modern furniture out of Kudu hide, bast meshing and chrome. Wooden decking on terraces invites guests to breakfast outdoors. A hidden spot to watch the wildlife is the outdoor shower.

Neue Maßstäbe im Hinblick auf Stil und Luxus setzt die intime Lodge am Sweni Fluss: Gläserne Wände umgeben sechs Suiten, die in sanften Khakitönen gestaltet sind. Der Effekt: die Grenzen zwischen den loftartigen Suiten und der Natur verschmelzen. Traditionelle Schnitzkunst, Tongefäße und Batikstoffe kontrastieren mit modernen Möbeln aus Kuduleder, Bastgeflechten und Chrom. Holz gedeckte Terrassen laden zum Frühstück im Freien ein. Ein versteckter Ort für Wildbeobachtungen ist die Outdoor-Dusche.

De nouveaux jalons en matière de style et de luxe se rencontrent dans le lodge intime bâti sur les rives de la Sweni : des murs en verre entourent les six suites décorées dans de doux tons kaki. Ainsi s'effacent les frontières entre les lofts et la nature. Les sculptures traditionnelles, les vases d'argile et les batiks contrastent avec les meubles modernes en cuir de koudou, en chanvre tressé et en chrome. Les terrasses de bois sont idéales pour le petit déjeuner en plein air. La douche en plein air est un endroit caché pour observer les animaux sauvages.

Este íntimo hotel situado a orillas del río Sweni, asienta nuevas bases en lo que al estilo y al lujo se refiere. Tabiques de cristal rodean las seis suites, decoradas en suaves tonos caqui. El efecto: los límites entre las suites, similares a lofts, y la naturaleza se funden. Tallas artísticas de madera, vasijas de barro y telas de batik, contrastan con los modernos muebles de cuero de kudu, mimbre y cromo. Las terrazas cubiertas con madera invitan a desayunar al aire libre. La ducha a cielo raso es un buen escondite para observar a los animales salvajes.

Nuovi criteri riguardanti stile e lusso propone il lodge familiare, ubicato al fiume Sweni. Pareti in vetro circondano 6 suites, arredate in morbidi toni khaki. L'effetto: i confini fra le suites – loft e la natura si avvicinano fino a fondersi. L'arte tradizionale della scultura in legno, vasi di terracotta e stoffe tinte con la tecnica batik contrastano con mobili moderni in pelle di Kudu, in rafia intrecciata e cromo. Terrazze ricoperte di legno invitano alla colazione all'aperto. La doccia outdoor è un buon posto d'osservazione per guardare attentamente gli animali selvatici.

Lounge, bathtub and terrace are front-row seats on Sweni River. From here, you can hear the Savannah's mysterious music.

Lounge, Badewanne und Terrasse sind Logenplätze am Sweni River. Von hier aus hört man die geheimnisvolle Musik der Savanne.

Le salon, la baignoire et la terrasse sont des endroits privilégiés sur les rives de la rivière Sweni. On y entend la mystérieuse musique de la savane.

El vestíbulo, la bañera y la terraza son los palcos a orillas del Sweni Rive. Desde aquí se puede oír la música de la sabana.

Il lounge, la vasca da bagno e la terrazza sono posti loggia allo Sweni River. Da qui si sente la misteriosa musica della Savana.

On the veranda, by the pool, in the Bush Spa and in the exclusive suites, you can relax and dream of exciting safaris.

Auf der Veranda, am Pool, im Bush-Spa und in den Nobelsuiten lässt es sich entspannt von aufregenden Safaris träumen.

Sur la véranda, au bord de la piscine et dans les luxueuses suites on peut rêver tranquillement à de palpitants safaris.

En la terraza, en la piscina, en el balneario y en las lujosas suites se puede soñar con los excitantes safaris.

Sulla veranda, nella piscina, nella Bush-SPA e nelle eleganti suites si può sognare rilassati degli eccitanti safari.

Singita Sweni Lodge *Kruger National Park, South Africa* 205

Royal Malewane

Hoedspruit, South Africa

Royal Malewane is a classic definition of what living and lifestyle culture means: a Victorian bath, prim antique furniture, candelabras, with white chaise-longues in Chesterfield style included. The owners have totally opted for colonial luxury. However, this style is combined with the origins of the wilderness: reed roofs, for instance, and exposed-beam ceilings. Individual immersion in the world of the game reserve is at the top of the list in the intimate atmosphere with only six suites and the Royal and Malewane Suites.

Royal Malewane definiert auf klassische Weise, was höchste Wohn- und Lebenskultur bedeutet: ein viktorianisches Bad, gedrechselte antike Möbel, Kronenleuchter, dazu weiße Chaiseloungen im Chesterfieldstil. Die Besitzer setzen ganz auf kolonialen Luxus. Der allerdings verbindet sich mit den Ursprüngen der Wildnis: Reet gedeckte Dächer etwa und offene Balkendecken. In der intimen Atmosphäre mit nur 6 Suiten sowie den beiden Royal und Malewane Suiten, steht das individuelle Eintauchen in die Welt des Wildreservats an vorderster Stelle.

Royal Malewane témoigne de façon classique de ce que signifie suprême culture de vie et d'habitat: salle de bains victorienne, antiques meubles tournés, lustres et chaises longues de style Chesterfield. Les propriétaires jouent à fond la carte du luxe colonial. Celui-ci est étroitement lié aux ressources du désert : par exemple, toits de chaume et plafonds aux poutres apparentes. Dans l'atmosphère intime des quelques six suites, ainsi que les Royal et Malewane Suites, l'immersion individuelle dans l'univers de la réserve est au premier plan.

Royal Malewane define de forma clásica el significado de una exquisita cultura de vida y de vivienda: un cuarto de baño victoriano, antiguos muebles torneados, candelabros y blancos sillones chaise lounge de estilo Chesterfield. Los propietarios apuestan por el lujo colonial, pero fusionándolo con los orígenes de la selva, como los tejados de caña y los techos de vigas. En las atmósferas íntimas, con solo seis suites y las Royal y Malewane Suites, lo más importante es la aproximación individual al mundo de la reserva.

Royal Malewane definisce in modo classico ciò che sono il vero gusto dell'arredamento e la vera arte di vivere: un bagno vittoriano, antique mobili lavorati al tornio, lampadari e bianchi chaise longue in stile chesterfield. I proprietari ci tengono al lusso coloniale in armonia con le origini della regione selvaggia. Come, per esempio, tetti fatti con la canna e soffitti a travi aperti. Così, en questa atmosfera intima, essendoci solo sei suites, e le Royal e Malewane Suites, immergersi nel mondo della reserva diventa una vera e propria esigenza.

Feel like the king of the bush veld—even if it's only at the fireside or enjoying an excellent dinner in a small group on the terrace.

Sich fühlen wie der König des Buschs – sei es nun am Kaminfeuer oder beim ausgezeichneten Dinner in kleiner Runde auf der Terrasse.

Se sentir le roi du bois – que ce soit au coin d'un feu de cheminée ou autour d'un dîner fin entre amis sur la terrasse.

Para sentirse como el rey de la selva, tanto al fuego de la chimenea como durante la exquisita cena en pequeños grupos en la terraza.

Sentirsi come il re della savana – anche se solo davanti al camino o desinando in compagnia di poche persone sulla terrazza.

So luxurious and as spacious as the king-size four-poster beds,—that's how the Victorian baths in the suites are also presented.

So luxuriös und geräumig wie die Kingsize-Himmelbetten präsentieren sich auch die viktorianischen Bäder der Suiten.

Aussi luxueuses et spacieuses que les lits à baldaquin king-size, les salles de bains victoriennes des suites.

Los cuartos de baños victorianos y las suites, son tan lujosos y espaciosos como las camas con dosel, de extraordinario tamaño.

Così lussuosi e ampi come i letti a baldacchino Kingssize si presentano anche i bagni vittoriani delle suites.

From the bed you can go right on to the terrace. At the very latest, guests enjoy a spectacular view from here.

Vom Bett aus geht es direkt auf die Terrasse. Und spätestens dort erwartet die Gäste ein grandioser Ausblick.

Du lit on rejoint directement la terrasse. S'offre alors une vue grandiose au visiteur.

Desde la cama el huésped puede dirigirse directamente a la terraza, donde le espera una grandiosa vista.

Dal letto si va direttamente sulla terrazza. E proprio dalla terrazza, al più tardi, gli ospiti possono godere di un grandioso panorama.

Earth Lodge

Sabi Sabi Private Game Reserve, South Africa

Like a chameleon, the clay rendered walls in the Eco Lodge fit in with the sand-colored surroundings. South African architect, Mohammed Hans, built them in the middle of the Sabi Sabi-Reserve, one of Africa's regions that are most densely populated by animals. The hotels interior presents itself extravagantly with specifically for the lodge created furniture such as tables with Impala horn legs and bathtubs that are reminiscent of giant, halved ostrich eggs. At dinner in the open loggia, the wilderness begins right in front of festively laid tables.

Wie ein Chamäleon passen sich die lehmverputzten Mauern der Eco-Lodge der sandfarbenen Umgebung an. Der südafrikanische Architekt Mohammed Hans hat sie mitten im Sabi Sabi-Reservat, eine der tierreichsten Regionen Afrikas, errichtet. Extravagant präsentiert sich das Interieur des Hotels mit einer eigens für die Lodge entworfenen Ausstattung wie Tische mit Impalahorn-Beinen und Badewannen, die an riesige halbierte Straußeneier erinnern. Beim Dinner in der offenen Loggia beginnt die Wildnis direkt vor der festlich gedeckten Tafel.

Comme le caméléon, les murs au crépi d'argile de l'éco-lodge se camouflent dans l'environnement couleur de sable. L'architecte sud-africain Mohammed Hans l'a placé au cœur de la réserve Sabi Sabi, l'une des régions les plus peuplées d'animaux d'Afrique. L'intérieur de l'hôtel se présente extravagant avec des meubles dessinés particulièrement pour la lodge comme des tables aux pieds en corne d'impala et des baignoires faisant penser á d'énormes demis œfs d'autruche. Au dîner sur la loggia en plein air, le désert commence en face des tables festivement dressées.

Los muros de adobe del lodge Eco se adaptan al entorno de color de la arena como un camaleón. El arquitecto sudafricano Mohammed Hans diseñó este hotel en medio de la reserva Sabi Sabi, una de las regiones con mayor fauna de África. El interior de la instalación se presenta extravagante con un amueblamiento diseñado especialmente para la lodge –como mesas con patas de astas de impala y bañeras parecidas a gigantescas mitades de huevos de avestruz. Durante la cena en la galería abierta, la selva empieza justo delante de la fastuosa mesa.

Come un camaleonte si adattano le mura con intonaco in argilla dell'eco-lodge all'ambiente circostante, che si presenta nei colori del deserto. L'architetto sudafricano Mohammed Hans ha eretto il lodge in mezzo alla riserva Sabi Sabi, una delle regioni più ricche d'animali. L'interno dell'Hotel si presenta stravagante con un arredamento particolarmente disegnato per il lodge come i tavoli con le gambe in corno di impala e le vasche da bagno, che richiamano la forma di gigantesche uova di struzzo dimezzate. Desinando nella loggia all'aperto, la vegetazione selvaggia della regione comincia direttamente davanti alla tavola festosamente apparecchiata.

Perfectly camouflaged: the bungalows are situated behind tall Acacias at a water hole where elephants quench their thirst.

Perfekt getarnt liegen die Bungalows hinter hohen Akazien an einem Wasserloch, wo Elefanten ihren Durst löschen.

Parfaitement dissimulés, les bungalows se dressent derrière de hauts acacias au bord du point d'eau où les éléphants viennent étancher leur soif.

Los bungalows se levantan, perfectamente camuflados, detrás de unas grandes acacias, a orillas de una laguna a la que los elefantes se acercan para saciar su sed.

Perfettamente mimetizzati, i bungalows sono ubicati dietro ad alti alberi d'acacia vicino ad una buca d'acqua, dove gli elefanti vanno a dissetarsi.

Beside the veranda, in the middle of a rock garden, safari guests can take a refreshing dip in the pool.

Neben der Veranda, inmitten eines Steingartens, können sich Safarigäste im Pool erfrischen.

A côté de la véranda, au milieu d'un jardin de pierre, les amateurs de safari se rafraîchissent dans la piscine.

Junto a la veranda, en medio de un jardín de piedra, los huéspedes del safari pueden refrescarse en la piscina.

Accanto alla veranda, in mezzo al giardino roccioso, gli ospiti del safari possono rinfrescarsi nella piscina.

214   Earth Lodge *Sabi Sabi Private Game Reserve, South Africa*

Behind the clay façade twelve luxury suites are hidden away. Cape Town designers created the reception area with native woods.

Hinter der Lehmfassade verbergen sich zwölf Luxussuiten. Den Empfangsbereich gestalteten Kapstädter Designer mit heimischen Hölzern.

Derrière leur façade d'argile se cachent douze luxueuses suites. Des designers originaires de Cape Town ont décoré la réception avec les essences locales.

Detrás de la fachada de adobe se ocultan doce suites de lujo. La zona de la recepción ha sido elaborada por diseñadores de la Ciudad del Cabo, que emplearon maderas autóctonas.

Dietro alla facciata in argilla si celano dodici suites di lusso. I designer di Città del Capo idearono i locali della ricezione con legno del luogo.

Index

Morocco

Marrakech **La Sultana**
Rue de la Kasbah, 40000 Marrakech, Morocco
T +212 (44) 388 008, F +212 (44) 387 777
www.lasultanamarrakech.com
21 luxury suites with internet access, air condition and fireplace. 2 restaurants, lounge bar. Meeting rooms. Panoramic rooftop-garden terraces (1.200 m² in total). Spa, hammams, sauna, gym, indoor Jacuzzi, outdoor heated pool. 3 golf courses nearby. 10 minutes drive from the airport.

Marrakech **Ksar Char-Bagh**
Palmeraie de Marrakech, BP 2449, 40000 Marrakech, Morocco
T +212 (44) 329 244, F +212 (44) 329 214
www.ksarcharbagh.com
12 harim suites with private garden or terrace and 1 apartment with private pool on its own terrace. Each accommodation with internet access, air condition. Heated pools, hammam, open air massage area, fitness center, tennis. Private airport transfer service.

Marrakech **Riad Enija**
9 Derb Mesfioui, Rahba Lakdima, 40000 Marrakech, Morocco
T +212 (44) 440 926, F +212 (44) 442 700
www.riadenija.com
7 rooms and 5 suites with private verandas. Kitchen serves meals on request. Situated in the Medina about 5 minutes walk from the Djemâa el-Fna square.

Egypt

Cairo **Four Seasons Cairo at The First Residence**
35 Giza Street, Giza, 12311 Cairo, Egypt
T +20 (2) 573 1212, F +20 (2) 568 1616
www.fourseasons.com
269 rooms and suites. Restaurant overlooking Cairo, Library Bar, Tea Lounge, poolside bar and grill. Open air pool on the fourth floor, health club, spa and wellness center. 45 minutes from Cairo International Airport.

Cairo **Conrad Cairo**
1191 Corniche El Nil, 11221 Cairo, Egypt
T +20 (2) 580 8000, F +20 (2) 580 8080
www.conradcairo.com
617 rooms and suites including 2 Royal and 2 Presidential Suites. 3 restaurants. Outdoor heated pool, health center. 11 meeting rooms, ballroom, casino. Located in the downtown area, 45 minutes from the airport.

Israel

Jerusalem **King David Hotel**
23 King David Street, Jerusalem 94101, Israel
T +972 (2) 620 8888, F +972 (2) 620 8882
www.danhotels.com
237 rooms including 37 Luxury Suites, 1 Presidential and 1 Royal Suite. 2 restaurants, bar and pool bar. Pool, tennis court, fitness center, massage. 20 miles from Ben Gurion International Airport.

Oman

Muscat **The Chedi Muscat**
North Ghubra 232, Way No. 3215, Street No. 46, Muscat 133, Sultanate of Oman
T + 968 (24) 524 400, F +968 (24) 493 485
www.ghmhotels.com
55 superior rooms, 60 deluxe rooms and 36 Chedi Club Suites with internet access. 2 restaurants, lobby lounge, 2 poolside cabanas. 2 pools, spa, private beach. 1 meeting room. 10 minutes drive from Muscat International Airport.

United Arab Emirates

Abu Dhabi **Emirates Palace Abu Dhabi**
Abu Dhabi West Corniche, P.O. Box 39999, Abu Dhabi, United Arab Emirates
T +971 (2) 690 9000, F +971 (2) 690 9999
www.emiratespalace.com
302 rooms, 92 suites including 4 Presidential suites. 4 restaurants, 3 bars. Private beach, 2 pools, spa. Auditorium, ballroom for 2.800 guests, 48 meeting rooms, business center. Marina. 30 km from Abu Dhabi International Airport.

Dubai **Beit al Bahar Villas**
P.O. Box 11416, Dubai, United Arab Emirates
T +971 (4) 348 0000, F +971 (4) 348 2273
www.jumeirah.com
19 villas with terrace and plunge pool. 2 restaurants, private dining available. Children's club and 4 pools at the Jumeirah Beach Hotel. Water sports, 3 squash courts, gym, yoga and karate, 7 tennis courts. Health suite. 30 minutes from Dubai International Airport.

Dubai **One&Only Royal Mirage**
P.O. Box 37252, Dubai, United Arab Emirates
T +971 (4) 399 9999, F +971 (4) 399 9998
www.oneandonlyresorts.com
The resort comprises 3 properties: The Palace (226 rooms and 20 suites with balcony or terrace), Arabian Court (162 rooms and 10 suites with balcony or terrace), Residence & Spa (3 Royal Villas, 18 suites and 32 deluxe rooms). 7 restaurants, beach bar, grill, rooftop bar, lounge. Health club, Spa, hammam. 20 minutes from Dubai International Airport.

Dubai **Madinat Jumeirah**
P.O. Box 75157, Dubai, United Arab Emirates
T +971 (4) 366 8888, F +971 (4) 366 7788
www.madinatjumeirah.com
Resort: Arabian village style, comprises 867 rooms and suites including 2 boutique hotels and 29 Traditional Courtyard Summer Houses. 45 restaurants. Spa, healthclub. Amphitheatre, conference facilities. 25 minutes from Dubai International Airport.

Dubai **Jumeirah Bab Al Shams**
P.O. Box 8168, Dubai, United Arab Emirates
T +971 (4) 832 6699, F+971 (4) 832 6698
www.babalshams.com
115 deluxe rooms including 10 suites. 2 restaurants, rooftop bar, pool bar and lounge. Different pool areas and shaded children's pool area. Spa. Meeting facilities. 45 minutes from Dubai International Airport.

Dubai **Al Maha Desert Resort & Spa**
Sheikh Zayed Road, Dubai, United Arab Emirates
T +971 (4) 303 4222, F +971 (4) 343 9696
www.al-maha.com
Built in the style of a traditional Bedouin encampment. 37 Bedouin Suites, 2 Royal Suites and 1 Emirates Suite. Dining room, lounge, bar, library. Spa and leisure center, pool. Conference facilities for up to 90 persons. 45 minutes from Dubai International Airport.

Seychelles

Frégate Island **Frégate Island Private**
Frégate Island, Seychelles
T +49 (6102) 501 321, F +49 (6102) 501 322 (Unique Experiences)
www.fregate.com
16 villas with terrace and Jacuzzi, 14 on top of the cliffs, 2 in private gardens. 2 restaurants, bar. 7 Private beaches, pool, gym, health club. Kid's club, baby-sitting service. PADI dive center, Hobie Cat sailing, guided hikes. 20 minutes from Mahé by private aircraft.

North Island **North Island Lodge**
North Island, Indian Ocean, Seychelles
T +248 293 100, F +248 293 150
www.north-island.com
11 villas with lounge, plunge pool. Each villa is equipped with an electro-buggy and 2 bicycles. Cuisine—each menu is created individually. Sunset beach bar. Spa with outdoor area. PADI dive center, gym. 4 beaches including a private honeymoon beach. 15 minutes from Mahé by helicopter.

Mauritius

Wolmar, Flic en Flac **Taj Exotica Resort & Spa, Mauritius**
Wolmar, Flic en Flac, Mauritius
T +230 403 1500, F +230 453 5555
www.tajhotels.com
65 villas with pool and al fresco dining area. All day dining restaurant, speciality restaurant and lounge bar. Swimming pool, spa, yoga pavilion. Sports center and tennis courts. 45 minutes from the airport.

Poste de Flacq **Le Prince Maurice**
Choisy Road, Poste de Flacq, Mauritius
T +230 413 9100, F +230 413 9130
www.princemaurice.com
89 suites including 12 Senior Suites (some with pool) and Princely Suite on the beach with garden/patio, 3 terraces and swimming pool. 2 restaurants, 2 bars. Two 18-hole championship golf courses. Health center, Guerlain Institute, massages. Squash court, gym, Jacuzzi, sauna, aerobics and yoga. 45 km from the airport.

Turtle Bay **The Oberoi Mauritius**
Turtle Bay, Pointe aux Piments, Mauritius
T +230 204 3600, F +230 204 3625
www.oberoihotels.com
73 villas in total including 2 Royal Villas with private pool, 23 luxury villas—16 of them with private pool—and 48 luxury pavilions. 2 restaurants, 3 bars. 2 swimming pools, spa, 2 tennis courts. Water sports. 55 minutes drive from Sir Seewoosagar Ramgoolam International Airport.

Tanzania

Ngorongoro

Ngorongoro Crater Lodge
Ngorongoro Conservation Area, Tanzania
T +27 (11) 809 4300, F +27 (11) 809 4400 (office Johannesburg)
www.ngorongorocrater.com
The lodge consists of 3 adjacent camps: North and South Camp with 12 suites each. Tree Camp with 6 suites. All accommodations with private viewing decks. Dining room with fireplace. Butler service. 1-hour drive from Olduvai.

Lake Manyara
National Park

Lake Manyara Tree Lodge
Lake Manyara National Park, Tanzania
T +27 (11) 809 4300, F +27 (11) 809 4400 (office Johannesburg)
www.ccafrica.com
10 tree house suites. En suite bathrooms and outdoor shower, overhead fans. Each suite with private game viewing deck. Meals are served in the open-air boma or the dining area. Private dining. Swimming pool. Flights to Lake Manyara airstrip followed by a 2 ½ hour game-drive to the lodge.

Namibia

NamibRand

Wolwedans
NamibRand Nature Reserve, Namibia
T +264 (61) 230 616, F +264 (61) 220 102
www.wolwedans.com
3 camps within a 10 km radius. Dunes Lodge: 9 chalets and 1 Mountain View Suite with kitchen. Main complex with pool, library, lounge. 2 dining rooms and wine cellar. Wooden walkways. Private Camp: 2 bedrooms, 2 bathrooms. Kitchen. Living room and lounge. Dune Camp: 6 tents on wooden platforms with private bathrooms. Main lodge with dining area and lounge. 90 km south of Sesriem/Sossusvlei. 15 minutes drive from private airstrip.

NamibRand

Sossusvlei Mountain Lodge
NamibRand Nature Reserve, Sossusvlei, Namibia
T +27 (11) 809 4300, F +27 (11) 809 4400 (office Johannesburg)
www.ccafrica.com
10 air-conditioned villas—each with private shaded veranda, in- and outdoor shower. Main complex with restaurant, bar, lobby lounge, guest areas, viewing deck and pool. Situated in the private NamibRand Nature Reserve. 10 minutes from the private airstrip.

Twyfelfontein

Mowani Mountain Camp
Twyfelfontein, Damaraland, Namibia
T +264 (61) 232 009, F +264 (61) 222 574
www.mowani.com
12 luxury tents with en suite bathroom and veranda, 1 luxury room with en suite bathroom and private terrace, 1 luxury suite with bedroom, lounge, in- and outdoor shower, terrace and private butler service. 1 restaurant, open air lounge, bar. Pool. 15 minutes drive from private airstrip.

South Africa

Cape Town

Cape Grace
West Quay Road, Waterfront, Cape Town, 8002, South Africa
T +27 (21) 410 7100, F +27 (21) 419 7622
www.capegrace.com
122 rooms and suites. Waterfront restaurant, bar, whisky bar and wine cellar. Spa. Communication center and meeting room. 20 minutes from Cape Town International Airport, 3 minutes from city center.

Cape Town

Mount Nelson Hotel
76 Orange Street, Cape Town, 8001, South Africa
T + 27 (21) 483 1000, F +27 (21) 483 1782
www.mountnelson.co.za
144 bedrooms and 57 suites including a 2 bedroom penthouse suite. 2 restaurants, afternoon tea in the tea lounge, on the terrace or in the garden. Planet Champagne Bar. 2 floodlit tennis courts. 2 heated swimming pools, bodycare center. 34 km from Cape Town International Airport.

Cape Town

The Twelve Apostles Hotel & Spa
Victoria Road, Oudekraal, Camps Bay, Cape Town, 8005, South Africa
T +27 (21) 437 9000, F +27 (21) 437 9055
www.12apostleshotel.com
55 rooms and 15 suites. Azure Restaurant, al fresco 24-hour Café, Leopard Bar & Lounge. Sanctuary Spa, sauna, fitness room, 2 swimming pools. Conference facilities for up to 90 persons. 40 minutes drive from Cape Town International Airport.

Hermanus

Birkenhead House
7th Avenue, Hermanus, Voelklip, 7200, South Africa
T +27 28 314 8000, F +27 28 314 1208
www.birkenheadhouse.com
11 suites—most of them with sea views. Dining room. 3 pools—one of them on dual levels. Spa, gym and treatment room. The whole hotel can be reserved for a maximum of 22 persons. Situated in Hermanus, 1 ½ hours drive from Cape Town.

Gansbaai

Grootbos Nature Reserve
P.O. Box 148, Gansbaai, 7220, South Africa
T +27 (28) 384 8000, F +27 (28) 384 8040
www.grootbos.com
23 suites with balcony, lounge and separate bedroom, airy bathroom. Restaurant, bar, lounge. Conference room for up to 60 delegates.

Montagu

Sanbona Wildlife Reserve
P.O. Box 149, Montagu, 6720, South Africa
T +27 (28) 572 1365, F +27 (28) 572 1361
www.sanbona.com
Sanbona comprises 2 lodges: Tilney Manor: 6 luxurious rooms with air condition, satellite television, private bar, fireplaces, freestanding baths, outdoor shower. Khanni Lodge: summer house with 4 suites, airy dining room, lounge with fireplace, outdoor dining patio. Private airstrip.

Plettenberg Bay

The Plettenberg
Look-out Rocks, P.O. Box 719, Plettenberg Bay, 6600, South Africa
T +27 (44) 533 2030, F +27 (44) 533 2074
www.plettenberg.com
38 air-conditioned rooms and suites. Lookout Villa (3 bedrooms) and The Beachhouse (2 bedrooms). Restaurant, cocktail bar, wine cellar. 2 swimming pools—1 of them heated. Spa, hammam. 15 minutes from Plettenberg National Airport (private charters only), 1 ½ hours from George Airport.

Plettenberg Bay

Tsala Treetop Lodge
P.O. Box 454, Plettenberg Bay, 6600, South Africa
T +27 (44) 532 7818, F +27 (44) 532 7878
www.tsala.com
10 suites with private plunge pool, sun deck fireplace. Dining room. Wooden elevated walkways between suites and main complex. Situated between Knysna and Plettenberg Bay, 5 hours from Cape Town. Small airport at Knysna and Plettenberg Bay.

Johannesburg

The Grace
54 Bath Avenue, Rosebank, Johannesburg, 2196, South Africa
T +27 (11) 280 7200, F +27 (11) 280 7474
www.grace.co.za
73 rooms including 10 suites and 3 one-bedroom penthouse suites on the top (10th floor)—each with en suite lounge, guest toilet, adjoining bathroom, separate shower and private balcony. Restaurant, vinotheque. Pool and spa.

Johannesburg

Saxon
36 Saxon Road, Sandhurst, Johannesburg, 2196, South Africa
T +27 (11) 292 6000, F +27 (11) 292 6001
www.thesaxon.com
24 suites including 3 Presidential suites with separate lounge and dining. Restaurant, dining library, cocktail bar and Cigar Lounge. Outdoor heated pool, Spa including 2 glass gazebos for sun tanning, 8 treatment rooms, beauty treatments, gym, yoga.

Johannesburg

The Westcliff
67 Jan Smuts Avenue, Westcliff, Johannesburg, 2193, South Africa
T +27 (11) 646 2400, F +27 (11) 646 3500
www.westcliff.co.za
80 rooms and 35 suites, most have private balconies. 2 restaurants, afternoon tea in the Polo Lounge. Terrace and bar. Function rooms and conference center for up to 150 people. Located in the select northern suburbs of Johannesburg.

Kwa Zulu Natal

Phinda Private Game Reserve
Maputaland, Kwa Zulu Natal, South Africa
T +27 (11) 809 4300, F +27 (11) 809 4400 (office Johannesburg)
www.ccafrica.com
Phinda comprises 6 lodges. Forest Lodge: 16 suites, swimming pool, dining and sitting areas. Mountain Lodge: 20 suites. Vlei Lodge: 6 thatched suites, dressing rooms, plunge pools and decks. Rock Lodge: 6 stone and adobe suites, sitting areas, decks and plunge pools. Zuka Lodge: 4 thatched bush cottages with verandas. Getty Lodge: 4 suites for exclusive use. Private airstrip.

Kruger Natl. Park

Singita Lebombo Lodge
Kruger National Park (southeast), South Africa
T +27 (21) 683 3424, F +27 (21) 683 3502
www.singita.co.za
15 luxury air-conditioned loft-suites with verandas, in- and outside shower. Various dining and living areas, wine cellar. Gym, spa, boma, swimming pool. 90 minutes flight from Johannesburg to Satara airstrip and from there a 40 minutes drive to the lodge.

Kruger Natl. Park

Singita Sweni Lodge
Kruger National Park, Sweni River, South Africa
T +27 (21) 683 3424, F +27 (21) 683 3502
www.singita.co.za
6 shaded suites with verandas, in- and outside shower. Dining room, wine cellar. Swimming pool, boma, gym and spa. 90 minutes flight from Johannesburg to Satara airstrip and from there a 40 minutes drive to the lodge.

Hoedspruit

Royal Malewane
P.O. Box 1542, Hoedspruit, 1380, South Africa
T +27 (15) 793 0150, F +27 (15) 793 2879
www.royalmalewane.com
6 suites with deck and private plunge pools, air condition and fireplace. Royal and Malewane Suites (210 square meters) for 4 guests in 2 en-suite rooms with private lounge, dining facilities, pool, private butler, chef and private game drives. Dining area. Library, gym and bush spa. 50 km from Hoedspruit.

Sabi Sabi

Earth Lodge
Sabi Sabi Private Game Reserve, South Africa
T +27 (13) 735 5261, F +27 (13) 735 5260
www.sabisabi.com
13 suites with plunge pool, in- and outdoor shower, air condition and telephone. Dining veranda and boma. Swimming pool. Wellness center, spa, treatments. Conference facilities with TV. 500 km east of Johannesburg. Private airstrip.

Photo Credits

Roland Bauer	La Sultana	14
	Ksar Char-Bagh	20
	Madinat Jumeirah	68
	Jumeirah Bab Al Shams	74
	Phinda Private Game Reserve	192
	Singita Lebombo	196
	Singita Sweni Lodge	11, 202
	Royal Malewane	206
	Earth Lodge	212
Tim Beddow	Ngorongoro Crater Lodge	116 - 119
Herbert Breuer	Wolwedans	126
Andreas Burz	Wolwedans	126
	Sossusvlei Mountain Lodge	130
	Mowani Mountain Camp	134
Michelle Galindo	Birkenhead House	150
	Grootbos Nature Reserve	156
	Tsala Treetop Lodge	172
	Saxon	182
Reto Gundli / zapaimages	Riad Enija	Cover, 26
Martin Nicholas Kunz	Four Seasons Cairo	
	at The First Residence	32
	Conrad Cairo	38
	Beit al Bahar Villas	60
	One&Only Royal Mirage	65
	Madinat Jumeirah	68
	Al Maha Desert Resort & Spa	80
	Frégate Island Private	86
	North Island Lodge	92
	Taj Exotica Resort & Spa Mauritius	98
	The Oberoi Mauritius	110
	Cape Grace	138
	Mount Nelson Hotel	143
	The Twelve Apostles Hotel & Spa	146
	Birkenhead House	150

	Grootbos Nature Reserve	156
	Sanbona Wildlife Reserve	162
	The Plettenberg	166
	Tsala Treetop Lodge	172
	The Grace	178
	Saxon	4, 182
	The Westcliff	188
	Phinda Private Game Reserve	192
	Jumeirah Bab Al Shams	7, 74
Heiner Orth	Lake Manyara	
	Tree Lodge	Backcover, 12, 120
Michael Poliza	North Island Lodge	92

Other photos courtesy

Cape Grace	Cape Grace	138
Conservation Corporation Africa (CCA)	Phinda Private Game Reserve	192
Constance Hotels & Resorts	Le Prince Maurice	104
Dan Hotels	King David Hotel	42
Earth Lodge	Earth Lodge	212
Four Seasons Hotels & Resorts	Four Seasons Cairo at The First Residence	32
Frégate Island Private	Frégate Island Private	86
GHM Hotels & Resorts	The Chedi Muscat	48
Kempinski Hotels & Resorts	Emirates Palace Abu Dhabi	8, 54
La Sultana	La Sultana	14
Ngorongoro Crater Lodge	Ngorongoro Crater Lodge	119 left
Taj Hotels & Resorts	Taj Exotica Resort & Spa Mauritius	98

Editor	Martin Nicholas Kunz & Patricia Massó
Introduction	Camilla Péus
Hotel texts by	Bärbel Holzberg (33, 54, 60, 68, 75, 80, 92, 98, 111, 126, 130, 134, 143, 197)
	Angelika Lerche (42, 156, 167)
	Camilla Péus (38, 86, 116, 120, 139, 151, 162, 172, 179, 182, 188, 192, 203, 212)
	Christiane Reiter (14, 26, 104, 146)
	Heinfried Tacke (20, 48, 206)
Layout & Prepress	Markus Mutz
Imaging	Jan Hausberg, Susanne Olbrich
Translations by	SAW Communications, Dr. Sabine A. Werner
English	Dr. Suzanne Kirkbright
French	Brigitte Villaumié
Spanish	Silvia Gomez de Antonio
Italian	Maria Angela Stella

Editorial project by fusion publishing gmbh, stuttgart . los angeles

www.fusion-publishing.com

Published by teNeues Publishing Group

teNeues Publishing Company
16 West 22nd Street, New York, NY 10010, USA
Tel.: 001-212-627-9090, Fax: 001-212-627-9511

teNeues Book Division
Kaistraße 18, 40221 Düsseldorf, Germany
Tel.: 0049-(0)211-994597-0, Fax: 0049-(0)211-994597-40

teNeues Publishing UK Ltd.
P.O. Box 402, West Byfleet, KT14 7ZF, Great Britain
Tel.: 0044-1932-403509, Fax: 0044-1932-403514

teNeues France S.A.R.L.
4, rue de Valence, 75005 Paris, France
Tel.: 0033-1-55766205, Fax: 0033-1-55766419

teNeues Iberica S.L.
Pso. Juan de la Encina, 2-48. Urb. Club de Campo
28700 S.S.R.R., Madrid, Spain
Tel./Fax: 0034-91-6595876

www.teneues.com

© 2005 teNeues Verlag GmbH + Co. KG, Kempen

ISBN-10: 3-8327-9060-8
ISBN-13: 978-3-8327-9060-8

Printed in Italy

Picture and text rights reserved for all countries. No part of this publication may be reproduced in any manner whatsoever.

All rights reserved.
While we strive for utmost precision in every detail, we cannot be held responsible for any inaccuracies, neither for any subsequent loss or damage arising.

Bibliographic information published by Die Deutsche Bibliothek.
Die Deutsche Bibliothek lists this publication in the Deutsche Nationalbibliografie; detailed bibliographic data is available in the Internet at http://dnb.ddb.de